Best wishes,

Jack Shaw

Through the Bible in Eighty Days

Jack Shaw

Through the Bible in Eighty Days

Jack Shaw

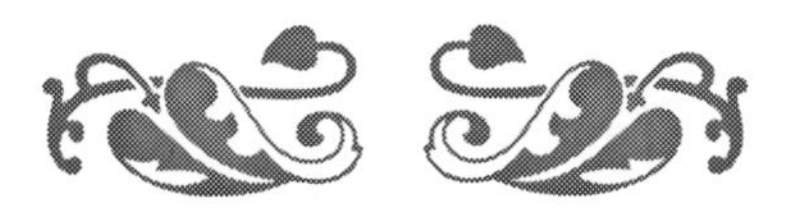

The **Hallamshire** Press
1994

For Joan and the children

First published in 1994 by
The Hallamshire Press

The Hallamshire Press is an imprint of
Interleaf Productions Limited
Exchange Works
Sidney Street
Sheffield S1 3QF
England

Typeset by Interleaf Productions Limited
Printed in Great Britain by
The Cromwell Press, Wiltshire

British Library Cataloguing in Publication Data
Shaw, Jack
Through the Bible in Eighty Days
I. Title
209

ISBN 1-874718-40-7

Contents

Acknowledgements

DURING my career as a college lecturer, I was fortunate to have many students who were broad-minded and inquisitive and did not let me get away with half-thought-out ideas and clichés. They did wonders to clarify my thinking. On a more practical level—and as far as this book is concerned—I am grateful to two students in particular: Kathryn Wilson, who typed my manuscript, and Paul Rowland, who, as well as playing left-back for my college soccer team with distinction, took some time to provide the illustrations.

Years ago Dr David Russell, my old Principal and a past General Secretary of the Baptist Union, first made biblical characters leap from ancient texts with surprisingly modern ideas, and I think my love affair with the Old Testament is due to him. I am grateful to Professor Philip Davies, from Sheffield University's excellent Biblical Studies Department, for reading the manuscript, and for his kind words in the Foreword.

Finally, I cannot speak too highly of the co-operation I have received from The Hallamshire Press. I have benefited enormously from their efficiency and know-how.

Foreword

THE Bible is not just a history book; it begins before Time and ends with a look beyond Time. But between these cosmic moments runs the story of the Jewish people and of the early Christians, which, claims the Bible, is also the history of the world as God sees it.

Our own civilisation was born from this remarkable story, and still draws deeply on it. Quite apart from its use in church (all too selective!) the Bible's heroes and villains romp through our literature and art, our language and imagination. We still see Abraham and David, Eve and Mary, Nebuchadnezzar and Daniel, Peter and Judas Iscariot, in our own and each others' deeds and experiences. Yet how many of us can say we know the Bible story as a whole well enough? In eighty episodes Jack Shaw has brilliantly retold that story in our own words—though he still lets the Bible speak for itself often enough. More importantly, he uses his knowledge, humour and wisdom to show how and why this story remains one that our own times should not neglect, because it can still tell us who we are.

Philip R. Davies
Professor of Biblical Studies,
University of Sheffield

How odd of God
To choose the Jews.

William Norman Ewer

Even Moses couldn't get along with the Jews.

Yiddish proverb

Beware of any people who say they are the chosen of history, or by God . . . They choose themselves. There are no Chosen People.

G.B. Edwards, *The Book of Ebenezer Le Page*

It is to the Jewish nation that humanity owes the deepest debt of gratitude, and it is on that nation that humanity has inflicted the deepest wrongs.

F.W. Farrar, Speech at Mansion House in 1882

Anti-Semitism is the final consequence of Judaism.

F.W. Nietzsche, *The Antichrist*, XXIV

Introduction

IMAGINE somebody sitting down to write a book in the days when Alfred the Great was King of Wessex and the Vikings were attacking East Anglia and Northumberland. Now imagine somebody else bringing that book to a close on the day Neil Armstrong walked on the moon and you will have some idea of the time-span involved in assembling the books we call the Bible. For it took something like a thousand years for that remarkable collection of literature to be gathered together in the form that we would now recognise.

People are still fascinated by this complex book which has done so much to develop the thinking of successive generations, but it is often read in such a haphazard way that the great sweep of its vision is lost. One of the reasons for this is that the Bible is not in chronological order; indeed sometimes within the same book are records from two or even three generations. Getting a real idea of historical progress therefore becomes very difficult.

Through the Bible in Eighty Days introduces us to the various characters who played a part in the developing saga that kept alive the idea that Israel was a chosen people with a special destiny. The stories indicate the social, political and economic backdrop against which they struggled with tyrants, temptation, ignorance and doubt. We meet people with great vision and faith, and others who were petulant, short-sighted and crass. In other words, the great story of the Bible is made up of many little pieces from people not unlike us. It must be so, otherwise the God who spoke to Moses has nothing to say to us in the atomic age.

This book has been written for the layperson and does not do justice to the complicated problems of biblical scholarship, though it certainly does not deny their wonderful work. It is hoped that readers will be sufficiently stimulated to delve deeper into these 'lively oracles of God' which have exercised people's minds and hearts for thousands of years.

Throughout the text the name 'Yahweh' is most often used to describe the God of the Jews. In English versions of the Bible, 'Yahweh' is usually translated 'the LORD'. Biblical references are from the New English Bible.

The Egyptians

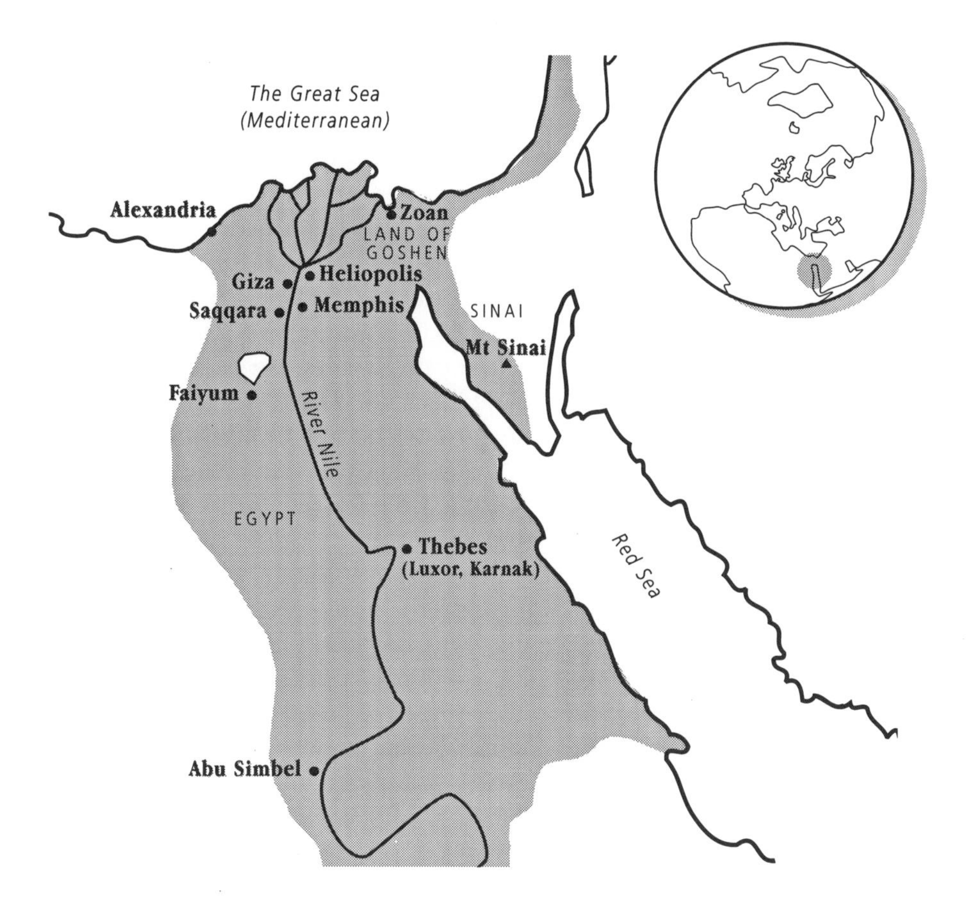

RIVERS are important features in the development of any society and civilisation, but this is especially true of Egypt, which owed its livelihood to the Nile and the ribbon of fertile land on its banks. Farming along the valley of the Nile goes back 6,000 years. The city-states, which dotted the banks, were united into a narrow kingdom and ruled by Pharaohs who were regarded as gods. The remarkable pyramids date back at least a thousand years before Abraham and were built as tombs for the Pharaohs. Khufu's pyramid is large enough to enclose six soccer pitches and has a square base which is constructed to within fifteen-millimetre accuracy!

Egypt's priests and nobles enforced the Pharaoh's laws and controlled the social order as well as agriculture and trade. Taxes were paid by farmers according to yield, which was of course dependent on the Nile. In normal circumstances the people ate well and enjoyed luxuries that were transported via the Mediterranean and the Nile. They were familiar with barley and wheat, fruit, and a wide variety of vegetables. As the Hebrews said after the Exodus: 'Think of it! In Egypt we had fish for the asking, cucumbers and water melons, leeks and onions and garlic. Now our throats are parched.' Wine was plentiful and beer was made from the barley. The priests and nobles were capable mathematicians, architects, scientists and engineers who had mastered the art of accurate surveying and were able to calculate that the year had 365 days. They built in great profusion and designed dykes and dams.

They were a religious people, as can be judged from 'The City of the Kings' near Luxor. Their two supreme gods were Ra, the sun god, and Osiris who was killed by his twin brother Seth, but resurrected with the help of his wife Isis. The Egyptians believed that bodies were essential in the afterlife and so they preserved them by a complex procedure of embalming and mummification, a process which reached its height about the time that David was forming his Israelite Empire.

The papyrus plant provided material for writing and a well-developed system of hieroglyphics enabled Egyptians to communicate easily. Jean-François Champollion, the French Egyptologist, deciphered the famous Rosetta Stone and provided the key to understanding the language. Today the words on the temples and monuments of Egypt can still be read.

It is generally accepted that the Hebrew exodus from Egypt took place during the period of the Hyksos dynasties and that the Pharaoh of the period who would 'not let my people go' was Rameses II of the nineteenth dynasty.

1 Abraham (c. 1460 BC)

Genesis 12–13; 19:1-29; 21:1-21; 22:1-19; Romans 4:1-23

ABRAHAM was born in Babylonia at a place called Ur on the Euphrates river—not all that far from the western border of present-day Iran. His father, Terah, was a nomad—a 'wandering Aramean'—and during his early years Abraham travelled with his father's tribe as it moved from oasis to oasis gradually migrating north. Five hundred miles north, the migrating stopped at a place called Haran, and here the community put down roots and settled.

Abraham never settled, however. As the community grew larger and the competition for space and food increased, so his wanderlust returned. By now he was the leader, the sheik, of the tribe and he felt compelled to move on. He believed that the great god El Shaddai was preparing his destiny. So one day, along with his nephew Lot, he uprooted all and they set off with their close families and possessions, westward towards the Mediterranean Sea and the fertile plains of Canaan.

He uprooted all and they set off with their close families and possessions.

The community, about three hundred in all, with black skin tents strapped to their camels, crossed the Jordan below a big lake, which years later was called Lake Galilee. Moving into Canaan, traditions say they stayed at places such as Shechem, Bethel and Hebron before moving to the Negeb and the edge of the Sinai desert.

At this point things went wrong. Lack of rain caused the oasis of the Negeb to dry up and in some desperation they moved into Egypt for help. Sadly, Abraham's courage and vision failed him and he became worried for his life. Abraham's wife Sarah was a very beautiful woman and he reasoned that when the Egyptians saw her they would kill him so that they could have her. They decided to pretend that they were brother and sister. Abraham's fears were well founded because the Egyptian Pharaoh did desire Sarah and took her into his harem. After some time, however, the truth came out and unceremoniously Abraham and his kin were sent packing back to Canaan.

The drought continued and it became evident that there were too many people and animals for the same land. So Lot and his family moved down to the fertile banks of the Jordan leaving Abraham in the less fertile valleys to the west. Lot rather unfortunately got himself mixed up with the sophisticated and perverted peoples of Sodom and Gommorah and only just escaped with his life when those cities were destroyed in a long-remembered holocaust.

Sarah had never given Abraham a child and she became so paranoid about it that she encouraged her Egyptian slave-girl Hagar to sleep with her husband. The plan worked. Hagar became pregnant and had a son they named Ishmael. Perhaps understandably, once Sarah saw the child she was consumed with jealousy and in a moment of waspish anger banished Hagar from the tribe, child and all. They fled to the desert, and tradition said that the child Ishmael was the founder of the fierce Ishmaelites who were 'real' nomads, living in the desert and raiding the cultivated regions.

When she was in middle age, Sarah did give Abraham a son whom they called Isaac. Obviously enough, they doted on him as the heir to the tribe of Abraham. But in those ancient days human sacrifice was not unknown and the strange idea played around in Abraham's mind that El Shaddai wanted his son as a sacrifice. On one horrific morning the idea became such an obsession that he almost killed Isaac. In time, he saw the stupidity of his feelings and sacrificed a ram instead.

It was Abraham who brought these wandering Arameans into Canaan, following a dream, a belief, that in this region he would become the father of a great nation. The sheik of a semi-nomadic tribe, he lived alongside the many Canaanite cities and customs but remained curiously aloof from them. Indeed, when he sought a wife for his son Isaac, it was back to Haran that he sent for Rebecca and not to the peoples of Canaan.

Abraham was a man with a dream, and how that dream was fulfilled is the saga of the history of Israel—and to some extent the history of us all.

*The Dome of the Rock, where Abraham prepared to sacrifice Isaac.**

* This is an Islamic building, because Abraham is also the forefather of the Arabs, who believe that Abraham prepared to sacrifice Ishmael on this spot on Mount Moriah.

2 *Jacob* (c. 1400 BC)

Genesis 25:19-34; 26:34-35; 27–35:1-15

JACOB was the son of Isaac and Rebecca and the grandson of Abraham. He had a twin brother called Esau and the pair of them were completely different. Esau was an outdoor type, a man of open plains, a hunter, whereas Jacob tended to hang around the tents philosophising or minding the animals. There was not much love lost between the pair of them. In fact, Jacob spent a good deal of time scheming about ways and means of getting Esau's inheritance from him. In those days the eldest son received a *double* portion of the inheritance and the priesthood or leadership of the family, and, as Esau had been born minutes *before* Jacob, he was technically the eldest.

Esau upset his parents by marrying two Hittite women instead of choosing from within the tribe. Jacob didn't make mistakes like that. Instead, with the help of his mother Rebecca, he tricked his blind and senile father Isaac into getting his blessing instead of Esau, and as a blessing once given could not be revoked he usurped Esau's place as elder brother. Naturally enough, Esau was angry and began to look for ways of killing Jacob. Without more ado Jacob left hurriedly and, again with help from his mother, made for Haran, where you remember Abraham and Rebecca his mother originated. His uncle Laban received him warmly, so Jacob stayed with him.

Laban had two daughters, Leah and Rachel, and Jacob, working hard to establish himself, eventually had enough money put aside to marry them both, though he loved Rachel much more than Leah. Still, Leah gave Jacob six sons, Rachel two, and in addition Leah and Rachel's slave-girls each bore him two. These sons, twelve in all, were given names which basically became the names of the later tribes of Israel.

There can be no doubt that Jacob was very astute, for soon his own sheep, camels, asses and slaves were as numerous as his uncle Laban's. As Jacob became more prosperous, so Laban's warmth cooled and Jacob was not slow to notice the change. He decided that he must return to his parents in Canaan, even though he knew he would have to face Esau again. In any case, deep down the hopes that had once inspired Abraham began to stir in Jacob too. He was to be a man of destiny.

He planned to leave Laban quietly and without fuss, but unfortunately Rachel stole her father's household gods before she left and this so infuriated Laban that he chased after them for seven days until he caught up with them in Gilead. But he couldn't find the gods and reluctantly let them go.

When the party arrived in Canaan, Jacob was scared at the thought of meeting Esau again. He was so worried that he divided his considerable herds, camels and sheep into four parties and sent them out one at a time to meet Esau. When they met him they were to say that they were presents from his brother. Jacob was obsequious, and really piled it on. Then as night came, Jacob, alone by the river Jabbock on the East of Jordan, sobbed out his fears to his god, El Shaddai. So fervent was his praying that night that later he could only describe the experience as 'wrestling with God'. It was an experience so intense that it changed his life. He even changed his name afterwards from Jacob to 'God strove' or more commonly 'Israel'.

The following day the meeting with Esau took place, and to Jacob's surprise his brother ran towards him and embraced him with tears. Esau was by now successful in his own right, the leader of a tribe, later called Edom, so his hatred had long since abated. Jacob now sought to establish himself in Canaan, co-existing with Edomites and other peoples of the region. He had some difficulties, notably with Hivites, one of whom, Shechem, raped Jacob's daughter Dinah. Simeon and Levi, his sons, were so incensed that they slaughtered the Hivites and for a while he feared reprisals, but it blew over and Jacob settled again. His religious fervour grew stronger with age and his faith never waned. He was convinced that one day, he, Jacob (or Israel as he was now called), would be the father of a great nation and that his twelve sons would be the foundation on which his dreams would be built.

3 Joseph (c. 1360 BC)

Genesis 37; 39–46:1-7; 47:27-31

JOSEPH was the second youngest son of twelve sons born to Jacob's wives and concubines. But he was the first son born to Rachel, Jacob's favourite wife and so he had a special place in Jacob's affections. Unfortunately, Jacob did not hide his special feelings for Joseph and this made the others jealous. Their jealousy was not helped by Joseph's tendency towards arrogance. He went too far one day and boasted that he had had a dream in which all the brothers were collecting sheaves in a field when Joseph's sheaf stood up and all the others fell down and worshipped it. Well, the significance of that story was not lost on the brothers and they hated Joseph all the more.

One day when the brothers were minding their father's flocks miles away in Dothan they ganged up on Joseph and shoved him into a pit. If it hadn't been for Reuben, the eldest, they would have killed him, but instead they daubed his gaudy coat with goat's blood and went back to their father with the news that Joseph was missing, presumed killed. Meanwhile, Joseph was being sold by wandering Ishmaelites to an Egyptian soldier called Potiphar who was the captain of Pharaoh's guard.

He did well in Potiphar's house. In fact the captain trusted Joseph so much that he soon put him in charge of his household. Then things went wrong. Potiphar's wife was infatuated with the good-looking Hebrew and tried to seduce him. When she met with rebuff after rebuff she concocted a story of attempted rape and Joseph was thrown into prison.

He proved to be an exemplary prisoner and soon had a reasonable amount of freedom within the Round Tower where he was imprisoned. He earned something of a reputation as an interpreter of dreams (a kind of ancient Freud), and managed to forecast correctly, through their dreams, the fate of a couple of Pharaoh's ex-employees. After two years or so this proved very useful. Pharaoh himself was troubled by perpetual dreams that nobody could explain. He constantly dreamed of seven fat cows grazing by the banks of the Nile when seven lean, hungry-looking cows emerged from the river and devoured the fat cows but didn't look any fatter afterwards. A similar dream concerned seven fat ears of corn consumed by seven thin ears. Joseph interpreted the dream to mean that Egypt was to enjoy seven years of good harvests and plenty but this would be followed by seven years of famine and scarcity. Joseph was even bold enough to suggest that a percentage of wheat should be set aside in the good years to provide for the bad.

Pharaoh was impressed by Joseph's acumen. So he appointed him Secretary of State and when Joseph's forecast proved to be uncannily accurate he became so influential that his authority extended throughout Egypt. He married a priest's daughter and had two sons, whom he called symbolically 'Manasseh' meaning 'to forget my hardship' and 'Ephraim' 'fruitful in his new land'. (These two names were later tribal names when Israel settled in Canaan.)

Anyway, Joseph's frugality proved so effective that soon the world was beating a path to Egypt's door to buy grain. Included in the flood to Egypt were Joseph's brothers, so hungry that they would grovel for bread. *And Joseph recognised them*. He withheld his identity for a long time, he toyed with them . . . played games with them . . . alternately fêted them . . . and accused them of theft.

However, he eventually became so emotional at the sight of his full-brother Benjamin and the thought of his father Jacob still alive that he revealed himself to them, and amid tears and rejoicing plans were made for Jacob (now called Israel) to settle in Egypt with his descendants and belongings. They lived in Egypt in a land called Goshen, in positions of privilege and honour because of the great influence of Joseph. *And that was how Israel and his family came to be in Egypt*. The stage was now set for the most momentous event in the history of the Jews

4 Moses and the Exodus (c. 1250 BC)

Exodus 2–6:13; 7:14–12:42; 14

THE descendants of Joseph and Jacob prospered in Egypt. Slowly their numbers became such that the Pharaoh began to see them as a threat. The multitudes mentioned in Exodus might be an exaggeration because there were only two midwives for all the Hebrew women, but there were enough of them to make the Pharaoh embark on a cruel policy of infanticide, which meant death for all the male Hebrew children.

But one boy escaped the slaughter and was raised in the Egyptian royal family as a prince. That child grew into manhood to become the greatest Hebrew of them all—Moses—a common enough Egyptian name but a far from common man.

Moses had to flee from Egypt when the Pharaoh hunted him following a skirmish with an Egyptian who died. He fled south towards the Sinai peninsula which pokes a rough triangle of land into the Red Sea, and there he stayed with the Midianite peoples. A priest called Jethro, a tribal leader of the Kenites, put Moses up and eventually gave him his daughter Zipporah in marriage. Jethro introduced Moses to the Kenite god of the hills, Yahweh, and this introduction was so momentous that it changed the history of the world.

Moses had never forgotten the sufferings of the Hebrews in Egypt. Their groanings reverberated in his own soul and he could not put them out of his mind. One day he was looking after Jethro's sheep near Mount Sinai (or Horeb—both the same) when his concern for the Hebrews and his faith in Yahweh met in a moment of religious fervour and insight. Whatever Moses saw in the burning bush was transformed into a religious sign. In this mountain rendezvous Moses had met Yahweh face to face and received a call that he was the chosen instrument to bring about the release of the captives in Egypt. From this moment on Yahweh was to be known as the 'God

Whatever Moses saw in the burning bush was transformed into a religious sign.

of Moses and Israel', the one who would be known by what he did.

Moses is at first reluctant to offer himself for the great task of freeing the Israelite slaves, but when at last he faces the Egyptian Pharaoh Rameses and demands that he 'let my people go', the drama builds up to a confrontation of great intensity. With his brother Aaron beside him, each visit to Pharaoh accentuates the crisis. Each Egyptian misfortune is used as proof by Moses that Yahweh is acting to release the slaves and each plague increases the gravity of the next meeting. In a truly remarkable way Moses convinced Rameses, *and the Hebrew people as well*, that Yahweh was acting in history to bring about his purpose. Moses' own sense of the immediacy of Yahweh's presence was transmitted to the Hebrew community with such persuasive passion that from then on Yahweh and Israel were to be bound together in a covenant or testament for all time.

Pharaoh Rameses did not give in easily. Despite the misfortunes that befell Egypt—the frogs, the maggots, the flies, the locusts and the hail—he held on grimly to his cheap Hebrew labour. But eventually when plague took away his eldest son his resolve gave way and he weakened. Moses at this moment of weakness organised the Hebrews and prepared them to leave the country. They were to be packed and ready to go at a moment's notice . . . and when that moment came, during the night, they left so hurriedly that the women had no time to wait for the yeast to leaven their bread, so they took the bread unleavened as it was.

Instead of heading north towards Canaan, Moses led the people south and east towards the Sinai mountains where he had first rendezvoused with Yahweh. But they had to cross the swampy Reed Sea, not far from where the Suez Canal is today, and it was here that the exodus reached its climax when the chariots of the pursuing Egyptian soldiers became bogged down in the marshes and the Hebrews could not be prevented from passing into the Sinai peninsula.

> *. . . and Miriam sang them this refrain:*
>
> > *Sing to Yahweh, for he has risen up in triumph;*
> > *the horse and his rider he has hurled into the sea*
> > **(Exodus 15:21).**

So the greatest event in the history of Israel came to a close. But it is still important to this day, for this exodus from Egypt was the springboard of Israel's faith. No, not 'was', but 'is', for without the Exodus experience, interpreted through the genius of Moses, Israel would never have been.

5 Moses the Law-Giver
(c. 1230 BC)

Exodus 16–20:17; 24:1-8; 33:1-11; 34:1-9; Numbers 13:17-33; 20:1-13; 21:10-35; Deuteronomy 34:1-12

FOLLOWING the dramatic exodus from Egypt, the Hebrews were led by Moses into the trackless wilderness of the Sinai peninsula, where, in that barren scrubland, they were to live for the next forty years. Travelling daily with their donkeys, goats and sheep they could cover some twelve miles every day until they came to a convenient water-hole. It was a bleak existence, shared by other wandering tribes and by Egyptian slave-gangs who dug for copper and turquoise in the Sinai mountains. There were skirmishes, notably with the Amalekites, who also sought water-holes for their animals.

At this juncture the leadership of Moses was seriously questioned. Faced with the scarcity of food and water, murmurings of discontent began to suggest that freedom in the desert was worse than slavery in Egypt. When things were at their worst a flock of exhausted quails flew into the Hebrew camp and were easily caught. These quails provided food in plenty and when this diet was supplemented by manna, a sticky substance secreted by insects (which Arabs still eat today), the murmurings subsided. Riding his luck (or was it sheer faith?) the indomitable Moses led the pilgrims on until they staggered into the oasis of Sinai, where at last they were able to set up their tents assured of water and provision.

In this mountainous oasis Moses taught the Hebrews to reflect on their experiences as a people. He showed them that their God, Yahweh, had called Israel into a relationship with himself—a covenant relationship. Under the shadow of Mount Sinai, Moses explained that Israel's children were to be people of Yahweh. *If they obeyed his laws.*

Jethro, Moses' father-in-law, whom you may recall had first instructed Moses in Yahweh worship, visited the Hebrews in Sinai and it was here that the *Laws of Yahweh* were clearly outlined. In a moral code so simple and profound, Moses explained that to keep the covenant with Yahweh Israel . . .

> *Could only worship Yahweh as God . . .*
> *Yahweh's name was to be revered . . .*
> *The seventh day of the week was to be a day*
> *of worship and recreation . . .*
> *In the community of Israel . . .*
> *Parents were to be honoured . . .*
> *Murder . . . adultery . . . stealing . . . lying . . .*
> *And jealousy were forbidden.*

These laws were now carved into the community's conscience for all time.

Moses was saying something nobody had said before—that Yahweh was concerned with the way people lived. He was concerned with the ethical life of the Hebrew community whose life was to be regulated by Yahweh's laws. After one awesome night of thunder and storm, Moses declared that these laws were now carved into the community's conscience for all time. They did not always keep the laws, of course—***but they knew what they were and they knew when they had broken them!***

After years of privation, hardship and moral training, the Hebrews were nearly ready to move into a homeland, which Moses said Yahweh would provide. He was still fighting a faction who dreamed of the cucumbers, melons and onions of Egypt. Indeed, he even had troubles in his own tribe of Levi, when Aaron and Miriam, his own brother and sister, plotted against him. But after long years of training Moses had moulded Israel's children into a community with a belief, a pattern of worship and a legal framework that was so good it can scarcely be bettered today.

Now the great leader revealed that Yahweh was to lead his people into the lush fertile land of Canaan. This was to be Israel's home—*and it flowed with milk and honey*. After the years of wandering no doubt it seemed that way.

Against the advice of Moses an abortive attempt was made to break into Canaan past the southern fortresses, but they were decisively repelled by Amalekites and Canaanite hill-peoples. So Moses took them on a long circuit past the southern shores of the Dead Sea to the well-known King's Highway. Here the Hebrews won their first major military victory. Now they were ready for a bold thrust across the River Jordan into the centreland of Canaan . . . and at this moment, with the promised land beckoning, Moses, the architect, founder and inspiration of Israel, died.

But his work lived on to shape the lives of us all.

The Canaanites

SOME time around 1900 BC in what is usually referred to as the Bronze Age, Iraq, Syria and Palestine were flooded with immigrants. A nomadic people called **Amorites** swarmed from the Arabian desert and settled in Mesopotamia. They were Semites with a distant ancestry that the Bible traces back to Shem, the son of Noah. It was an ancestry they shared with Babylonians, Arameans, Assyrians, Canaanites and, of course, present-day Jews and Arabs. By 1750 their influence had spread to Syria and Palestine. It is possible that Abraham was among these migrants since many of his relatives—Peleg, Serug, Terah, Haran and Benjamin—have the same names as those found on 20,000 Mari tablets discovered in 1935 and dating back to this Amorite invasion.

Other immigrants filtered into the land from the Caucasian mountains of Armenia in the north. The Old Testament calls them Horites, but they are usually called **Hurrians**, and the Egyptians did actually call Palestine the land of the Hurru for a period. Also moving from the north were the **Hittites** looking for milder river valleys than they had known near the Russian steppes. They had mastered the use of iron and therefore had a considerable advantage over the surrounding people still using bronze. They had developed a code of law similar to that of the Babylonian Hammurabi.

Into the territory north-west of Israel came the Canaanites, also known to us by their Greek name, **Phoenicians**. They were mariners whose ships visited every part of the Mediterranean coast. Their chief ports were Tyre and Sidon, though other ports included Berytus (Beirut) and Byblus. Interestingly, Egyptian papyrus passing through this port became known as 'Byblus' which eventually gave us the word 'Bible'. The Phoenicians later founded the great city of Carthage in present-day Tunisia, which became so important in the later development of Rome. They worshipped the god 'El', the highest god of the Canaanites and most of the Semitic peoples (note the number of times *el* appears in names such as Isra*el* and Ezeki*el*). Beside El stands the young god Baal, the god of fertility, who proved to be so seductive to the Israelites.

Later settlers were the **Philistines**, sea peoples from the Aegean, and wanderers called **Habiru**, whose roots in the land were very shallow, allowing them to move onward in times of famine. Some people link these wanderers with the Hebrews.

What is clear from these migrations is that the time we refer to as 'the partriarchal period' was a time of great upheaval and tribal movement. When the book of Exodus describes Palestine as 'the land of Canaanites, Hittites, Amorites, Perizzites, Hivites and Jebusites', it is not exaggerating. The disparate nature of this migration meant that 'the land of Canaan' was filled with disparate peoples. Consequently, Israel's struggle for the land became a series of battles against independent city-states who, although described as 'giants living in walled cities', lacked the unity necessary to resist a determined invader.

6 Joshua (c. 1200 BC)

Joshua 1–11; 24

MOSES, the architect and inspiration of the Hebrews, was succeeded by his commander Joshua. Joshua's task was to complete the work of Moses and establish the largely nomadic people in a land of their own.

The task was more complicated than the later editors of Israel's traditions suggest. At first reading it appears that Joshua in three masterly campaigns into the centre, south and north of Canaan completely destroyed all opposition, leaving the Hebrews in control of the whole land within a few months. A truly remarkable *blitzkrieg*, especially as their weapons were crude and the Canaanites had chariots of iron!

What Joshua actually did was to launch an attack on Jericho from across the River Jordan. Taking advantage of shallow waters caused by an up-river landslide, he crossed the river quickly and besieged the ancient city. The siege lasted a week. The Hebrews believed that Yahweh was fighting on their behalf to provide them with a land, but this did not stop Joshua planning. By clever use of spies he ascertained that people inside the fortress walls of Jericho were sympathetic to them. Among these were the family of Rahab the prostitute. Consequently, Joshua began his attack, knowing full well that a fifth column existed within the city ready to spring to his aid at a moment's notice. He then subjected the people of Jericho to enormous psychological pressure. Silently circling the walls of the city on six successive days they put the fear of Yahweh into the inhabitants. Then, in a pre-arranged signal, soldiers blasted on their horns and shouted their head off. This was the moment for the gates to be thrown open from inside. The besieging army rushed in and mopped up the demoralised defenders in one of the quickest and most decisive of military victories. The city was burned to the

Then, in a pre-arranged signal, soldiers blasted on their horns.

ground and the inhabitants massacred according to the ancient custom of *cherem*. Nothing was kept as plunder, everything had to be destroyed in an act of total purification. Tradition says that one man, Achan, did help himself to booty but he paid with his life when he was discovered.

Joshua's army had now proved itself in battle and looked round for other vulnerable city-states—and there were plenty. In the south Egypt was riddled with internal strife and unable to offer protection. In the north Assyria was still a sleeping giant. The hilly terrain of the land left communities isolated, and it was these that Joshua decided to pick off. He was not reckless enough to challenge Canaanite chariots on the plains, but his troops were well suited to hill fighting and in a brilliantly conceived ambush he defeated the city of Ai (some scholars think it was actually Bethel) and subjected them to *cherem*. Moving south he was confronted by a confederation of five Amorite kings whose intention was to stop the Hebrews once and for all. They failed. In blizzard conditions, which nullified Canaanite chariot power, Joshua outmanoeuvred his rivals and broke the resistance. Hail blotted out sun and moon for twenty-four hours causing the triumphant soldiers to sing:

> *Stand still, O Sun, in Gibeon;*
> *stand, Moon, in the Vale of Aijalon* **(Joshua 10:12)**.

Gaining in confidence, Joshua's army pressed on southward adding Lachish, Hebron, Debir and Eglon to their triumphs. They even ventured to the coastal region and had success at Gaza.

The biblical record reads:

> *So Joshua massacred the population of the whole region—the hill-country, the Negeb, the Shephelah, the watersheds—and all their kings. He left no survivor . . .* **(Joshua 10:40)**

Flushed with success, he moved north, still wise enough to avoid the impregnable Jerusalem.

In the region of what was later Galilee, he stormed and took Hazor the huge capital of the district. Only since the archaeological discoveries of Yigael Yadin in the 1950s has it become clear just how impressive Hazor really was. Standing in two hundred acres and sheltering 30–40,000 people, it provided some of the best living conditions of the ancient world and was Canaan's largest city. Joshua's achievement was considerable. Nevertheless, it was exaggerated by later writers who claimed that he had conquered *all* the land. They ignored the fact that Philistines occupied the coastal plains, the Jebusites remained secure in Jerusalem, Canaanites lived in Gezer and the tribe of Manasseh made no headway around Megiddo. Other tribes formed alliances with the people of the land and later intermarried with them. The region around Shechem is not mentioned as a battleground at all, which might suggest that the region was already populated by kinsmen of the Hebrews. Joshua's great work was that he gained a substantial foothold on the promised land's hilly regions which was a large step in the transformation of his people from nomads to a settled community.

After conquest came the task of allocating land to the tribes, some of whom had roots going back to the exodus from Egypt, while others had joined the federation later. It was a loose federation of twelve tribes sometimes called an amphictyony. They did not always see eye to eye and their needs and fears were very different. What bound them together was an allegiance to Yahweh, the God of Moses and to the saga of Hebrew history. Even kinsmen who allied themselves to the invaders later accepted the saga as their own, just as American states did when they joined the Union after the fight for independence from Britain. At Shechem the allegiance to Yahweh was renewed, probably annually. The great deeds of Yahweh were related and his moral laws repeated. He was exalted as their 'saviour God' who had called the Hebrews to be Israel, his people, but he was a jealous God who needed re-dedicated lives and pure living.

However, the gods of Canaan would not die easily and the battle for the minds of the people had yet to be won.

7 Local Heroes (Judges) (c. 1150 BC)

Judges 1–3

THE years immediately after Joshua were unsettled years. There was no dominant power throughout Canaan. Israel's tribes were established in influential pockets of land, but Canaanites still lived around them and sometimes *with* them. Nomads attacked the tribes for plunder, neighbouring peoples such as the Moabites were often hostile, as were the sophisticated Philistines who were settling in coastal regions on the Gaza strip. It was an uneasy period of transition, not unlike that in Anglo-Saxon England after the departure of the Romans. Local heroes sometimes sprang up to deal with particular threats but Israel had no central political authority and no charismatic leaders of the quality of Moses and Joshua. The religion of Yahweh and the saga of Israel's beginnings were still unifying factors but were not, in themselves, capable of fusing the tribes into a nation.

It was a period of anarchy and uncertainty. The exploits of local heroes were remembered in song and legend and occasionally laboriously written down, to be incorporated many years later into the Israelite saga. The names of these heroes flit tantalisingly before our eyes in the book of Judges—Shamgar, Tola, Elon, Abdon and Ibzan—whose exploits have been condensed to the absolute minimum:

> *. . . Ibzan of Bethlehem was judge over Israel. He had thirty sons and thirty daughters. He gave away the thirty daughters in marriage and brought in thirty girls for his sons. He was judge over Israel for seven years, and when he died he was buried in Bethlehem* **(Judges 12:9-10)**.

Brief sentences of the achievements of Othniel were remembered and then included in both Joshua and Judges, including a strange detail about his wife's flatulence! Othniel was a southerner from

Judah but he was also credited with the distinction of ridding northern tribes of the oppression of a Mesopotamian king from around Syria (Joshua 15:17; Judges 1:13).

A more informative legend surrounds the person of Ehud. The Moabites on the eastern shores of the Dead Sea had grown strong and were in a position to dominate neighbouring Israelite tribes who had to pay protection money to the fat Moabite king Eglon. This unhappy situation persisted for eighteen years. Then Ehud, a left-handed Benjamite, decided enough was enough. Going to Moab to pay tribute he first made a short two-edged sword and hid it

Ehud plunged the fifteen-inch blade into Eglon's voluminous belly.

under his clothes on the right-hand side. Security was slack and the sword went undetected. Having paid his tribute, Ehud made an excuse to go back to Eglon, privately offering him a gift. As the fat king's lips quivered in anticipation of the gift, Ehud reached across himself and plunged the fifteen-inch blade into Eglon's voluminous belly. The murder went undetected for some time because the servants thought their king had locked himself in the toilet! Meanwhile, Ehud rallied men from Ephraim who attacked the fords on the Jordan controlled by Moabites and killed thousands, thereby reversing the power positions of Israel and Moab.

The stories in Judges are not edifying in the slightest, but they are fascinating insights into the fluctuating fortunes of the tribes in their early days of settlement. Judges is not history in the modern sense of the word and is not a chronological record of events. Indeed, some of the heroes could well have been contemporaries.

Four hundred and fifty years after the exploits of the local heroes, Jewish religious reformers went through the legends in Joshua and Judges and worked out a theological theory, which was:

> ***Whenever Israel worshipped Yahweh sincerely and solely, they were blessed with peace and prosperity. When they slipped in their allegiance they were punished by oppression and grief.***

This theory became orthodoxy and eventually all the Jewish law, history and saga were edited to underline the belief. We call these editors Deuteronomists or writers of the Second Law, and their orthodoxy flavours all Old Testament scripture. It is still possible to see within Joshua and Judges that fraternisation between Israel's tribes and the Canaanites did take place,

> *. . . the Israelites lived among the Canaanites, the Hittites, the Amorites, the Perizzites, the Hivites, and the Jebusites. They took their daughters in marriage and gave their own daughters to their sons; and they worshipped their gods* **(Judges 3:5-6)**.

Later generations saw this syncretism as the root cause of all Israel's misfortunes.

8 Deborah (c. 1140 BC)

Judges 4–5

ESTABLISHING themselves in Canaan meant more for Israel's tribes than simply keeping enemies at bay. There was also a living to be scratched from the soil by people new to the art and rigour of farming. The struggle for food absorbed time and energy. Meanwhile Canaanite city-states began to re-assert themselves. The strong chain of Canaanite cities which had remained untouched by Israel's invasion moved onto the offensive. Their formidable chariots dominated some of the plains and restricted communication and trade between Israel's tribes. The result was:

> *. . . caravans plied no longer;*
> *men who had followed the high roads*
> *went round by devious paths* **(Judges 5:6)**.

There was a real danger that some Israelites might become isolated from the federation and fall easy prey to aggressive Canaanites. An outstanding influence on Israel at this time was a prophetess called Deborah who lived in the central hill-country of Ephraim. The term 'judge' is accurate with regard to this woman because she used to sit under a well-known palm tree and listen to the disputes of the people. She was well respected and her justice was fair and well received. She was one of the few people of the day to have a finger on the co-operate pulse of Israel's life and she was a devout daughter of Yahweh. Information was fed to her that life was very difficult indeed for tribes that had settled in the north. Joshua had conquered the great city of Hazor but a king called Jabin had established himself there and was harrying the tribe of Naphtali. Jabin's commander in chief Sisera, was a particular thorn in the side because he had control over a formidable chariot force. Naphtali was incapable of withstanding these chariots alone and desperately needed assistance from other tribes in the federation.

Deborah's achievements have been preserved by two sources, one in prose and the other in song, and the song is very valuable because it is probably contemporaneous with the events described. It shows quite clearly that when Deborah sounded the clarion call in the name of Yahweh, calling all the tribes to come to the assistance of Naphtali, the response was mixed. Ephraim, the warlike Benjamites, Zebulon and Issachar responded positively to the call with men and resources but Reuben was split and in the end chose to continue farming rather than get involved. Manasseh too stayed across the Jordan. Even Dan and Asher, neighbouring tribes of Naphtali, refused to support Deborah's call to action and preferred to 'tarry by the ships' and 'linger by the sea shore'.

Deborah decided that Barak from Naphtali should lead an assault on Sisera's troops, but he would only go if Deborah went as well. She went and eventually the opposing forces met on the slopes of Mount Tabor, which was just as Deborah had planned it. On the hilly terrain, Barak's army, equipped with the home-made weapons of farmers, were irresistible. Chariots were spilled over and heavy rain demoralised the Canaanites and trapped their retreat by swelling the River Kishon.

The stars fought from heaven,
the stars in their courses fought against Sisera.
The Torrent of Kishon swept him away,
the Torrent barred his flight . . . **(Judges 5:20-21)**

Sisera himself left his chariot and fled from the battle on foot. Shattered and fearful he came across a Kenite tent (remember the Kenites first introduced Moses to the mountain god Yahweh) and accepted hospitality from a woman called Jael. She inveigled him into her tent, fêted him, relaxed him and, when he eventually dozed off to sleep, she split his skull open with a hammer and tent peg. Deborah's song finishes with a pitiful picture of Sisera's mother waiting for her son to return from battle.

The mother of Sisera peered through the lattice,
through the window she peered and shrilly cried,
'Why are his chariots so long coming?
Why is the clatter of his chariots so long delayed?
. . .
'They must be finding spoil, taking their shares,
a wench to each man, two wenches,
booty of dyed stuffs, for Sisera' **(Judges 5:28-30).**

Deborah and Barak saw off the threat of the Canaanite kings once and for all and hastened the merging of Israel and Canaan into one people. One people, but, as yet, not united under allegiance to one God.

9 Gideon (c. 1130 BC)

Judges 6–8

ANOTHER threat to the Israelites at this time was that of marauding Bedouins or Midianites who swept into Canaan from the Arabian desert. These people were not greedy for land but for food. When the tribes were ready to harvest the fruit of their labour, marauding bands on camels scoured the countryside stealing and uprooting crops. Like a swarm of locusts they turned fertile fields into a wasteland. In Ephraim and Manasseh especially, conditions were so bad that families were driven out of their homes in fear and lived in caves, dens and mountain retreats.

One day a young man of Manasseh, whose brothers had been killed by these Midianites, was hurriedly threshing wheat in the seclusion of the winepress, hoping to salvage a little from the predators. His name was Gideon (another tradition calls him Jerubaal) and as he worked, the scandal of Israel's plight appalled him. They were working for nothing and living in constant fear for their lives. As with Moses, generations before, the conviction grew that he could be 'the man for the hour'. Gideon's religious ideas mixed up Yahweh and the Baals and it seems likely that Yahweh was worshipped alongside his father's altar to Baal. But it was Yahweh who was calling for Gideon's allegiance. If the Midianites were to be prevented from pillaging the land he was the one to act and his action would be in the name of Yahweh, the God of Moses.

His first deed was to declare his religious conviction. In trepidation and the secrecy of darkness he chopped down his father's sacred poles to Baal and overturned the altars. It was very nearly the last thing he did. The citizens were so incensed by the vandalism that had his father Joash not defended him vehemently, they would have killed him. But Gideon's colours were now pinned firmly to Yahweh's mast and when the Midianites, joining with Amalekites and other nomads from the east, ostentatiously crossed the Jordan and camped in the lush vale of Jezreel, it was in Yahweh's name that Gideon called the tribes of Israel into action. Messengers were sent to Asher, Zebulon, Naphtali and throughout his own tribe of Manasseh. The response was so good that Gideon's initial deference soon changed to confidence and even arrogance.

Gideon had a superb plan to rout the Midianites. Central to his idea was an elect SAS type of force, three hundred strong, whom he chose for their recklessness and fearlessness, typified by the uninhibited way they drank their fill at the water-holes. These three hundred were to creep undetected to the perimeter of the Bedouin camp at night, taking with them jars and trumpets. Meanwhile, as the camp was being approached by the three hundred, other troops were taking up their positions at other strategic places such as fords on the River Jordan, entrances to gullies and vantage points. The plan relied on strict military precision. Gideon waited until the Midianites changed their middle watch, then, in the uncertainty of that moment, he blasted on his trumpet and smashed his jar. The elect force followed his action to a man shouting:

. . . *'For Yahweh and Gideon!'* **(Judges 7:18)**

Fires were lit simultaneously to add to the confusion. Within minutes the Bedouin camp was in pandemonium. In complete bewilderment they struck out against each other in the darkness, then, when they fled the camp in straggling disarray, they were picked off easily by the remaining Israelite troops. Belatedly, the tribe of Ephraim had to be called into action to cut off the Midianite retreat to the south. They resented being called into action in what was simply a mopping-up operation, but Gideon pacified them.

The victory was complete and total. Bedouin chiefs were rounded up and killed, including Zebah and Zalmunna who had killed Gideon's brothers. The scourge of the Midianites had been eradicated.

Gideon's achievement was greeted with unalloyed thanksgiving. He was fêted as the Saviour of Israel and many wanted his leadership extended to overall ruler of Israel, but like some early-day Caesar he refused a crown for himself and his sons. Instead he melted down gold from the booty of conquest and erected a statue in his home town of Ophrah, which in later years became a place of pilgrimage. Gideon spent the rest of his life in affluence, gratifying himself with a large harem and concubines that produced seventy legitimate sons.

Unfortunately, there was a serpent in the nest.

10 Abimelech (c. 1110 BC)

Judges 9

GIDEON had won the respect of his own tribesmen and it was a respect that stretched to other tribes as well. Nevertheless, the years following his death illustrate perfectly why the dream of an overall leader for all Israel's tribes was met with wary reservation. There was a hope that the magical charisma of Gideon might live on in his sons and produce a firm dynasty of rule for the northern tribes at least. It was a forlorn hope.

The harem of Gideon produced seventy sons, but there were in addition offspring from other sexual liaisons. One of these children was called Abimelech. He was an 'illegitimate' son to a married slave-mistress who lived in Shechem, the large town where years before Joshua had called the tribes to dedicate themselves solemnly to Yahweh. There had never been any political ambition in Gideon and consequently he had not sought to build up a following in the larger towns, being content to live in his father's small township of Ophrah. After Gideon's death it was Abimelech who exploited the political vacuum by whipping up support for himself in a bold thrust of power. His mother's clan supported him and several of his half-brothers put his case by hint and innuendo to the leading citizens of Shechem. These citizens offered financial assistance and soon Abimelech was able to surround himself with a coterie of roughnecks, who in an orgy of violence massacred Gideon's sons.

Only Jotham, the youngest, survived and he, by subtle speeches from Mount Gerazim, couched in Mark Antony-style language, kept the treachery of Abimelech before the public conscience. Had they been fair to the memory of his father? Did his family deserve such fate? Was the son of a slave-girl worthy of kingship? Jotham's rhetoric did not win the day and he fled for his life but his words were long remembered, especially a fable he told about trees desiring a king to rule over them. Useful trees such as the olive, the fig and the vine all refused the honour and they finally settled for the prickly, inflammable bramble, a decision which would consume them all in flames!

It took three years for the kindling to light. Abimelech had sown the wind, he would reap the whirlwind. Lawlessness begat lawlessness. Bands of men ganged together. One gang led by Gaal, son of Ebed, was in open hostility with Abimelech and sought opportunity to usurp his position. As outlaws they terrorised the countryside, robbing and pillaging. Gaining in confidence they entered Shechem in Abimelech's absence and went into a drunken carousal which filled the citizens with terror. For protection some allied themselves with Gaal believing Abimelech to be impotent. Zebul, the governor of the city, was not one of these and when the outlaws were sleeping off the effects of a boozy session, messages were sent to Abimelech clearly spelling out the situation. He was not slow to respond.

By morning as Gaal and his cronies were still throwing up over the city walls, Abimelech and his forces were swarming over the hills towards them. Still half-drunk they didn't realise the weakness of their position, and when Zebul taunted them with cowardice they rode out into the open plain to confront Abimelech. They were routed. The roads outside Shechem were strewn with corpses all the way to the entrance of the city itself.

Abimelech, however, was not satisfied. He regarded Gaal's insurrection to be evidence of treachery inside Shechem and began a welter of destruction. Panic-stricken city leaders and their wives locked themselves in the great hall of Baal's temple, seeking respite from the avenging angel of death. Their respite was short-lived. In deadly earnest he kindled a huge fire and burnt the temple to the ground, incinerating men and women with impunity. Then, while the fires of hatred were burning so fiercely, he marched his soldiers fifteen miles to Thebez seeking other victims in his purge. The residents took refuge in their strong castle, bolting the doors and scampering to the rooftops. Once again Abimelech prepared to burn the castle to the ground, and when all was ready he stooped to light the holocaust. Then fate played his hand. A woman on the roof of the castle, with more optimism than precision, heaved a millstone off the roof. It struck Abimelech squarely on the head and fractured his skull. He lay on the ground writhing in agony, screaming for his armour-bearer to kill him and save him from the ignominy of being killed by a woman.

So the armour-bearer ran him through and the traumatic years of Abimelech were over. Israel had tasted kingship and the bitterness of the experience would not easily be forgotten.

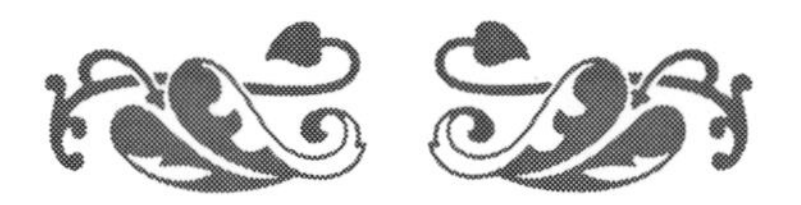

11 Jephthah (c. 1100 BC)

Judges 11–12

THE tribes of Israel had been saved from enemies on the eastern side of the Jordan by Ehud and Gideon. Now Ammon, also from 'across the river' began acting aggressively towards Gilead. One of Gilead's noblemen was blessed with several children, including a son called Jephthah who was born out of wedlock to a prostitute. As the nobleman's sons grew older they steadily ostracised Jephthah until he was forced out of his father's house and went to live among the people of Tob. Here he became recognised as the leader of a large gang of notorious freebooters. As with Joseph years before, a day would dawn when Jephthah would enjoy a day of reckoning.

As the bellicose posturing of the Ammonites increased, so the people of Gilead grew more fearful until their nobles had to go, cap in hand, to Jephthah asking for his help. They believed that he was the only one with sufficient charisma and skill to lead the people's resistance to Ammon and so they promised Jephthah almost everything he asked. He made it clear he wanted nothing less than lordship over Gilead and complete control over the tribe's forces. The tables had been well and truly turned. Jephthah did not venture into battle immediately. Diplomacy was attempted, but when the talking degenerated into the reciting of old prejudices and mythological injustices, Jephthah prepared for war.

Following the custom of his day he first had to ascertain whether Yahweh really wanted the battle and could guarantee victory. He prayed at Yahweh's shrines for hours but the skies were leaden and no assurances came to him. In desperation he sought a Faust-like bargain with his God.

> *'If thou wilt deliver the Ammonites into my hands, then the first creature that comes out of the door of my house to meet me when*

I return from them in peace shall be Yahweh's; I will offer that as a whole-offering.' **(Judges 11:30-31)**

The assurance Jephthah had sought flooded through him. Yahweh, he was certain, had accepted the bargain.

Brimful of confidence, Jephthah crossed the Jordan and attacked the Ammonites who collapsed like a house of cards. City after Ammonite city fell until the whole nation was completely subdued. Only then did Jephthah rest his sword.

But when Jephthah came to his house in Mizpah, who should come out to meet him with tambourines and dances but his daughter, and she his only child; he had no other, neither son nor daughter. When he saw her, he rent his clothes and said, 'Alas, my daughter, you have broken my heart, such trouble you have brought upon me. I have made a vow to Yahweh and I cannot go back.' **(Judges 11:34-35)**

Neither did he go back. Unlike Abraham and Isaac there was no later vision and Jephthah's daughter was duly sacrificed. She lived on in the memory of her people —proof that Israel's history was not entirely uncontaminated by human sacrifice and a saint of virgins who honoured her memory on four days of every year.

In the aftermath of victory the belligerent tribe of Ephraim remonstrated with Jephthah for not including them in his battle plans, just as they had done with Gideon years before. This time, however, Ephraim was not pacified with gentle words and tribal warfare broke out. Gilead routed Ephraim and controlled the fords over the Jordan.

When any Ephraimite who had escaped begged leave to cross, the men of Gilead asked him, 'Are you an Ephraimite?', and if he said, 'No', they would retort, 'Say Shibboleth.' He would say 'Sibboleth' [they had trouble with their sibilants], and because he could not pronounce the word properly, they seized him and killed him at the fords of the Jordan **(Judges 12:5-6)**.

This inter-tribal feuding was a sad omen of things yet to be.

12 Samson (c. 1050 BC)

Judges 13–16

THE stories of Samson are different from other stories in Judges. They do not deal with a military leader so much as a womanising strongman whose exploits in boudoir and tavern kept the gossips of the day well fed with material. The stories bring us for the first time face to face with the Philistines, who were settling into Canaan at the same time as the Israelites and establishing themselves in the west on the shores of the Mediterranean. They were sea-people with a well-developed culture and were masters at producing iron weapons and tools. Building cities such as Gaza, Gath and Ashdod, they were a formidable threat to Israel's tribes, and ironically Canaan was later called Palestine after them. They were to torment Israel for many generations, though during Samson's days their strength had not been fully realised.

Samson was born to aged parents from the tribe of Dan who occupied the Shephelah district before Philistine pressure made them migrate northwards towards the Syrian border. They were so delighted to have a belated son that they dedicated him to Yahweh as a Nazirite, just as John the Baptist's parents did over a thousand years later. He was not to drink strong wine, shave his head or go near corpses lest he should be defiled. But Samson was not a moral or religious giant. His name became synonymous with strength and violence and he was reputed to have killed a lion with his bare hands.

While still a young man he became infatuated with a Philistine woman in Timnath and, though his parents desired an Israelite girl for their son, he insisted on marrying her. Alas, the marriage festivities became a fiasco. Samson gambled the whole of his marriage dowry on a foolish riddle, the answer to which was promptly passed onto Philistine lords by his bride-to-be. In a fury Samson paid off his debts by murdering thirty Philistines and stealing their clothes.

In retaliation the woman was married off to Samson's groomsman. Predictably, this enraged Samson even more and he burnt fields of Philistine corn and destroyed their vineyards and olive groves.

By this time Samson was an embarrassment to the Israelites who were suffering from Philistine reprisals as a direct result of his rashness. In desperation, men of Judah captured Samson, bound him and handed him over to the Philistines. Alas for them, their joy was short-lived. Snapping the ropes that bound him, the Israelite strongman picked up the jawbone of an ass and using it as a cudgel beat up a gang of Philistine youths. His remarkable slaughter was remembered in a song.

> *With the jaw-bone of an ass I have flayed them like asses;*
> *with the jaw-bone of an ass I have slain a thousand men*
> **(Judges 15:16)**.

Thereafter, Philistines tried to kill him on his frequent excursions into their whorehouses, but his phenomenal strength always enabled him to escape.

Strength and good fortune could not protect him forever, though, and when he fell in love with a *femme fatale* called Delilah his tragic demise could not be long delayed. She was in league with Philistine lords who sought the source of his great strength. The man from Dan did not have many moral scruples, but he did believe that Yahweh had given him his gift of strength, symbolised by the long hair which denoted the Nazirite dedication to Israel's God. When Delilah hoodwinked him and shaved off his hair, Samson was so demoralised that the Philistines captured him easily. With ruthless zeal they gouged out his eyes and imprisoned him in Gaza where they committed him to forced labour grinding their corn.

In the solitude of prison the foolishness of his past came home to him like slap in the face and he re-dedicated himself to Yahweh. His hair grew and he abstained from wine. Slowly his self-confidence returned and strength flowed through his body once again.

His hatred of Philistines unabated, he awaited an opportunity to be avenged for the loss of his eyes. The opportunity was not long in coming. At a great religious sacrifice to their god Dagon, the Philistines drank themselves legless and thought they would increase their fun by ridiculing their fallen adversary Samson. He was led from the dungeons by a young boy who left him leaning on the main pillar of the temple. The lords taunted him. In a tremendous surge of Herculean energy, Samson dislodged the central pillar and brought the roof of the temple crashing down, burying him among the Philistines he hated so much.

Samson's story is tragic in that it tells of a man who misused his remarkable gifts and lost his vocation in the perfumed flesh of women. More importantly for Israel, it heralds the beginning of a prolonged struggle with the Philistines for domination of the Promised Land.

In a tremendous surge of Herculean energy, Samson dislodged the central pillar.

13 Eli (c. 1070–1020 BC)

Judges 17–19; 1 Samuel 1–4

THE rakish lifestyle of Samson was symptomatic of what was happening to Israel's tribes. With the exception of Dan, they had settled into definite areas of land, but the moral rigour that had sustained them and been their life's blood in Moses' day had eroded into lethargic superstition. They were lawless times when murder, theft, sodomy and gang rape were commonplace. The Ten Commandments were relics of the past, and the book of Judges says succinctly:

> *In those days there was no king in Israel and every man did what was right in his own eyes* **(Judges 17:6)**.

As if to illustrate how bad things were, Judges tells of an Ephraimite called Micah who had his own household gods presided over by a Levite (the tribe of Levi were priests without tribal land of their own). As the Danites moved northwards away from the Philistines, they had no compunction about stealing Micah's gods and his Levite as well. Might was right. In another story, a travelling Levite with his concubine is passing through Gibeah in Benjamite land, and is given hospitality in an old man's home. Louts in the town try to break down the door in an attempt at buggery on the Levite and in the end sexually abuse the concubine to such an extent that she dies. Appalled, the Levite cries,

> *'Has the like of this happened or been seen from the time the Israelites came up from Egypt till today?'* **(Judges 19:30)**

The terrible deeds of the Benjamites were greeted with abhorrence by the other tribes who attacked them. Then, having defeated them, they each took a solemn oath that none of their daughters would ever marry into the tribe of Benjamin. It was some years before

Benjamin's infamy was forgiven, and even then their tribal oaths were only overcome by a rough compromise that allowed the lusty bucks of Benjamin to marry virgins from Jabesh-gilead. Then, when there were too few virgins to go round, a blind eye was turned in their direction when they carried off the maidens of Shiloh in a kidnap reminiscent of the Roman rape of the Sabine women.

In the midst of the moral anarchy, an old priest called Eli sought to preserve the religion of Yahweh, the God of Moses. He presided over a house that had been dedicated to Israel's warrior god at Shiloh. Faithful pilgrims still made annual visits to Shiloh to offer sacrifices, but even here corruption had spread its clammy hand and contaminated Eli's sons, Hophni and Phinehas. Their sexual appetites had become a byword and, in contravention of ritual law, they ran a racket that enabled them to extort all the succulent morsels of meat from sacrifices offered by the pilgrims. Yahwehism became contemptible.

Also in the House of Yahweh at Shiloh was the Ark of the Covenant, which had been an integral part of Yahweh religion since Moses' day. The Ark was a wooden, rectangular chest which had stood inside the tent where Moses had kept his rendezvous with Yahweh in the wilderness. According to tradition, the Ark contained the Ten Commandments inscribed on stone. Yahweh was the invisible God but the Ark represented his portable throne, and when it was carried into battle on two long poles thrust through the top of the chest, it was an assurance that Israel's God was present, 'tabernacled' with his people. In preserving the Ark and officiating over the sacrifices, Eli kept the tender plant of Yahwehism alive. But even Eli was powerless to prevent the next peril to befall Israel.

The Philistines had begun to expand their muscles. Judah and Benjamin had no answer to their superior weapons and organisation, and Dan migrated northward. This left the tribe of Ephraim directly threatened. A showdown was inevitable and it took place between Ebenezer and Aphek, not far from present-day Jaffa. The Israelites were comprehensively defeated. In panic they complained that Yahweh had not protected them and raced off to fetch the Ark from Shiloh to the battlefield.

> *When the Ark came into the camp all the Israelites greeted it with a great shout, and the earth rang with the shouting. The Philistines heard the noise and asked, 'What is this great shouting in the camp of the Hebrews?' When they knew that the Ark of Yahweh*

had come into the camp, they were afraid and cried, 'A god has come into the camp. We are lost!' **(1 Samuel 4:5-7)**

Even with the Ark the Israelites were crushingly defeated. Thousands of foot soldiers died, Hophni and Phinehas were killed and the Ark was taken.

The priest Eli, ancient and blind, anxiously awaited news of the conflict, and when a battered survivor from the fray returned with news of the catastrophe, the old man fell off a gate and broke his neck. In accord with these disastrous times, Phinehas's widow bore a son who was named 'Ichabod', which meant 'Glory has departed from Israel'.

So it seemed. The tribes were in disarray, the Philistines reigned supreme and the word of Yahweh was seldom heard. In these desperate days, a young man was growing to maturity in the sacred shrine of Shiloh. His name was Samuel and he was the greatest Israelite since Moses.

When the Ark came into the camp all the Israelites greeted it with a great shout.

14 *Samuel* (c. 1040–1000 BC)

1 Samuel 1–12

FOLLOWING terrible defeats at the hands of the Philistines, the star of Israel was fading fast. Their troops were no match for the cock-a-hoop enemy, who started pushing into the hill-country and increasing pressure on the tribes. Cities were sacked and destroyed, among them the ancient shrine of Shiloh. The later book of Jeremiah and archaeological evidence both indicate a destruction so complete that rebuilding was out of the question.

Israel's pitiable decline was witnessed at first hand by Samuel, a trainee priest who assisted the old man Eli at Shiloh, having been left in Yahweh's service by his pious parents Elkanah and Hannah. (The syllable 'ah' from Y*ah*weh was often incorporated into Hebrew names as was 'el' from the ancient god El.) Samuel had seen with his own eyes the priestly abuses of Eli's sons, the corruption of Yahwehism, the death of Eli, the loss of the Ark and the destruction of Shiloh. He had tasted the bitterness of despair and yet had retained his faith in Yahweh, the God of Moses, and still believed that Israel was His people chosen and called. His life's work was to convey this belief to shattered Israelites who, even after the return of their Ark, were still smarting under Philistine oppression.

> *No blacksmith was to be found in the whole of Israel, for the Philistines were determined to prevent the Hebrews from making swords and spears. The Israelites had to go down to the Philistines for their ploughshares, mattocks, axes and sickles to be sharpened. The charge was two-thirds of a shekel for ploughshares and mattocks, and one-third of a shekel for sharpening the axes and setting the goads* **(1 Samuel 13:19-21)**.

Our knowledge of Samuel comes from at least two sources and has been further edited by later generations, but his influence on the life of Israel at this period is undisputed. He is regarded as a prophet, a fortune-teller, a priest, a judge and, most important of all, as a kingmaker. In the person of Samuel all the features of Israel's future development take root, and under his spiritual leadership Yahweh faith showed the resilience and vitality necessary to make recovery possible.

From Dan in the north to Beersheba in the south, Samuel's name was respected as a prophet. Then, after the destruction of Shiloh, Samuel moved the centre of his operations to the Ramah/Mizpah region where he began a circuit dispensing justice in the hill-country of Ephraim. As priest he offered the sacrifices for his people and prayed constantly on their behalf. In the hurly-burly of his punishing schedule two convictions took shape in his thinking. They were, first, that Israel could never be strong and resourceful as a people until they believed in Yahweh with the bottom of their hearts as well as the top of their heads, and, secondly, they could never be truly united until they were led by a king capable of commanding the loyalty of *all* the tribes of Israel. If the immediate burden of Philistine oppression was to be lifted and the future assured, these two conditions had to be fulfilled.

It was the second of these conditions that was revolutionary. Israel had never regarded herself as a nation at all but as *a people* linked as a community to a common religious saga. Each tribe coveted its own independence. If they had a king there might come a day when he would turn into a tyrant and make Israel's sons fight his battles and Israel's daughters serve in his harem. The examples of tyrants from surrounding nations was a stern reminder of what could happen. Furthermore, there was an inherent contradiction in Samuel's idea of a king. Surely Yahweh was supposed to be Israel's king? Why then was an earthly monarch necessary? The arguments for and against monarchy are clearly expressed in the book of Samuel, but sources are confused as to how strongly Samuel felt himself. Nevertheless, something had to be done. Philistine domination was irksome in the extreme and if it was ever to be overthrown Samuel was the one to initiate that overthrow.

Legend tells of how a personable young man called Saul, head and shoulders above his compatriots, went out one day searching for lost asses, ran into Samuel the prophet and instead found a kingdom. Another story has him hiding behind baggage as Samuel seeks to advocate his kingship. Both stories agree that Saul was Samuel's choice as the first king of Israel. Some were pleased to have him and cried, 'Long live the King!' Others sceptically asked, 'How can this fellow deliver us?' Saul's own bravery and leadership in delivering the town of Jabesh-gilead from the Ammonites swung things his way and he was duly and solemnly appointed king, with Samuel explaining to all the conditions of monarchy.

Samuel had significantly changed the course of history. Although he had second thoughts about his choice of king, Israel had become a nation, like the other nations. It was a fateful decision which started tremors that are still causing earthquakes in the twentieth century.

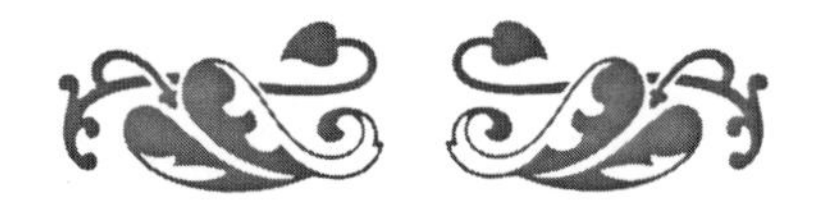

15 Saul (c. 1020–1000 BC)

1 Samuel 10–31

SAUL had been chosen by Samuel as the first King of Israel, an honour he accepted without enthusiasm. Inter-tribal jealousy made the achievement of unity seem unlikely, especially for a man coming from the small tribe of Benjamin. But Saul was not without charisma and soon began to win over those who lacked faith in him and the new regime. An opportunity to show his prowess came early. The Ammonites had always been a thorn in the side of those tribes east of the Jordan, and though they had been subdued by Jephthah years before, they were now making aggressive moves against Jabesh-gilead.

> *. . . Nahash the Ammonite attacked and besieged Jabesh-gilead. The men of Jabesh said to Nahash, 'Come to terms with us and we will be your subjects.' Nahash answered them, 'On one condition only will I come to terms with you: that I gouge out your right eyes and bring disgrace on Israel'.* **(1 Samuel 11:1-2)**

Not having much room for compromise, a delegation was sent to Saul's home in Gibeah and he responded immediately by circulating all the tribes with a call to war. The response was magnificent, even Judah mustering men to send to the fray. Nahash was overwhelmed and annihilated and the strength of Ammon completely broken. Furthermore, Saul's ability to fuse tribal volunteers into a successful army made a profound impression on the waverers who enthusiastically renewed their allegiance to Saul and the monarchy in a joyous celebration at Gilgal.

Israel had tasted the power that unity could bring and they savoured the moment. In Samuel and Saul, priesthood and monarchy came together bringing oneness to the federation, and Saul even allied himself to the ecstatic prophetic movement. The fusion of religious and political ideals bred a national confidence which suggested that

Israel would soon be capable of tackling the running sore in her side—the Philistines. Hostilities were not far away. Saul's son Jonathan was in charge of a third of the new army stationed at Gibeah, and one day he killed a Philistine governor. News spread among the Philistines that the Hebrews were in revolt. Saul sounded the trumpet throughtout the land and farmers and fishermen rushed to join the regular soldiers by Saul's side at Gilgal. Days of subjection and phoney peace were over: at last confrontation was to take place.

The battle was fierce, with fortune fluctuating throughout and death becoming so familiar that the initial ardour for war was soon quenched. Nevertheless, Jonathan, by sheer audacity, achieved a brilliant victory at Michmash and for a period the pressure of the Philistine oppression was lifted in Ephraim and Benjamin. The war was not won, but Israel did have a breathing space and the time to attend to marauding Amalekites whom they slaughtered in a blood bath.

However, all was not well. The unity of purpose could not be sustained and the alliance of religion and politics was short-lived. Samuel's relationship with Saul became strained when the old prophet/priest accused the king of usurping his priestly role. Saul pleaded his innocence but Samuel was not convinced. Then, following the battle with the Amalekites, Saul was reprimanded for not applying the sacred *cherem* and destroying all the spoils of war. Saul claimed he had and Samuel replied sarcastically, 'What then is this bleating of sheep in my ears? Why do I hear the lowing of cattle? Desperate to placate the holy man, Saul grabbed the old man's cloak which ripped away in his hand. Samuel spun round and, pointing dramatically at the king, cried,

> *'Yahweh has torn the kingdom of Israel from your hand today and will give it to another, a better man than you.'* **(1 Samuel 15:28)**

Agag, King of the Amalekites was hewn in pieces by Samuel and the *cherem* ruthlessly applied. From that day to the day of his death, Samuel never saw Saul again.

National unity had proved to be a pipe dream, and though Saul continued as king his initial fervour began to evaporate. Strong and brave men were still conscripted into his services but long bouts of depression plagued him. One soldier, skilled with the harp, was employed to soothe Saul's temper at this time and he became the king's constant companion, forming an indissoluble friendship with his son Jonathan and marrying Saul's daughter, Michal. The soldier's name was David, and Saul loved him; his promotion was well received by officers and people alike. David's popularity increased until eventually Saul began to see this attractive young man as a threat to himself and his dynasty. He grew jealous of David's popularity which was fanned when he heard women singing:

> *Saul made havoc among thousands*
> *but David among tens of thousands* **(1 Samuel 18:7; 21:11).**

Saul's warm feeling for David cooled rapidly and he tried to kill the young pretender. He would have done so had it not been for Jonathan who helped to organise David's escape from his father's clutches.

Saul's latter years were a sad end to what had promised to be a great life. Philistine wars continued and Saul's early successes were not maintained; fear of David never left him and much of his energy was dissipated pursuing his *bête noire* through wilderness and hill country. His dispute with religious leaders continued, culminating in a shameful murder of Yahweh's priests at Nob. Saul became miserably isolated. In desperation he sought consolation from a witch of Endor who conjured up the spirit of Samuel but, as with Macbeth, there was no antidote for his despair.

> *Blow wind, come wrack;*
> *At least we'll die with harness on our back* **(*Macbeth*, Act 5, Scene 5).**

So might Saul have cried, for in his final battle against the Philistines on Mount Gilboa his army was over-run. Saul himself, severely wounded by archers, fell on his own sword and killed himself. Three of his sons, including Jonathan, were among the dead. The Philistines in triumph decapitated the royal corpses and nailed their bodies onto the walls of Bethshan. Brave men from Jabesh-gilead fondly remembered the way a younger Saul had liberated their city in happier days, recovered the royal bodies and buried them decently within their city.

The first king of Israel was dead and the dark clouds of oppression once again banked ominously in the sky. But the star of David was climbing the heavens and would not be denied.

16 David the Outlaw
(c. 1010 BC)

1 Samuel 16–31; 2 Samuel 1–4

GREAT men attract legends, and there are so many surrounding David, the son of Jesse from Bethlehem, that it is not always easy to separate fact from fantasy. According to one source, Samuel had already anointed David for kingship before the young shepherd forced himself onto Saul's attention by killing Goliath, the formidable fighting champion of the Philistines. Another source says that David was introduced to Saul as a skilled soldier-cum-musician who had the ability to ease Saul's depressions. It could be this same source that tells us that Elhanon, the son of Jair from Bethlehem, was the man who killed Goliath (2 Samuel 21:18-22). Perhaps, just as the witty remarks of others have sometimes been attributed to Winston Churchill, so might the heroic deeds of others have been attached to David, the greatest of Israel's kings.

Be that as it may, it is certain that David joined Saul's court as a young man, soon struck up a firm friendship with Jonathan, the king's son and married Michal, the king's daughter. Such was the personal attraction of the man that he soon outstripped Jonathan and Saul in public esteem and women sang songs about him. Saul was not slow to see danger in David's popularity—not so much for himself, but for Jonathan, fearing that public opinion might wrest the crown from his offspring in favour of the son of Jesse. The king determined that David had to die, but such was the young man's charm that Jonathan and Michal were prepared to forsake personal ambition to ensure that he did not fall into their father's hands. With artful guile they engineered his escape from court.

David and a few faithful friends were now fugitives. The priests of Nob were tricked into helping David by supplying food for his men, and when Saul found out they paid for it with their lives. With danger facing him in every village, David fled to the Philistines at

Gath but they were understandably suspicious of him and he had to feign madness to escape. He hid in the cave called Adullam in the border hill-country of Judah and here he was joined by his family and others who had a grievance against Saul. He became the leader of an outlaw band of four hundred men, and, having secured the safety of his parents by finding a place for them in the court of the king of Moab, he trained his gang of mercenaries. His following increased and included Abiathar, the one priest of Nob to elude Saul's blood bath. They raided settlements such as that at Keilah where Philistines were killed and their cattle stolen. Like some Chicago gangster he grew rich from protection money, and when this protection was refused by a wealthy landowner called Nabal he did not see the light of many more days. Nabal's beautiful widow Abigail was shrewd enough to marry David with haste, increasing his personal wealth and prestige in the process.

There was a price on David's head throughout these outlaw days. Saul harassed him, gave his daughter Michal to a man called Paltiel and tried to capture him whenever he got a report of a sighting. But David was fed with information from Saul's court and outmanoeuvred him to such an extent that he twice had the king at his mercy but refrained from killing Yahweh's anointed. When Saul increased the pressure, the outlaws once again went to the Philistine king, Achish of Gath, who reasoned that a renegade Israelite band could be useful in his struggle against Saul. Fortunately for David, he was never required to fight against Israel and was not on the field when Saul and Jonathan fell in the tragic battle of Mount Gilboa. He was genuinely distressed by their deaths:

Weep for Saul, O daughters of Israel!
who clothed you in scarlet and rich embroideries,
who spangled your dress with jewels of gold.

. . .

I grieve for you, Jonathan my brother;
dear and delightful you were to me;
your love for me was wonderful,
surpassing the love of women (**2 Samuel 1:24-26**).

Grief at the Gilboa tragedy could not disguise the fact that the political situation was now ideal for David to make a thrust for power. He had ingratiated himself with both Philistines and the tribe of Judah, where he had protected landowners from robbers and liberally showered around the booty from his many raids. He moved his family and friends, lock, stock and barrel, to the city of

Hebron in southern Judah, and here the elders of the tribe came to him and pronounced him king. The northern tribes were not so accommodating and east of the Jordan at Mahanaim, Abner, Saul's chief army commander, made Saul's remaining son Ishbaal king of the north. ('Bosheth', meaning 'shame', later replaced 'baal' in the name to suit the religious position of editors.) Ishbaal was little more than a puppet manipulated by Abner, but it is significant that for seven years the claims of David were resisted by the northern tribes. Indeed, had it not been for the treachery and intrigue of the military, it is doubtful whether David would have achieved the position of king of all Israel.

17 Joab and Abner
(c. 1000–960 BC)

2 Samuel 2–4

DAVID'S commander-in-chief was Joab, the son of David's half-sister Zeruiah. He was a ruthless opportunist but, along with his younger brothers Abishai and Asahel, was completely dedicated to David. He was the king's hatchet man and could be relied on to do any dirty work that needed doing, even working on his own initiative if he believed it to be in the king's best interests. The relationship between king and commander was prickly and often hostile, but nobody understood David better than Joab, and his influence on the king was considerable.

Abner was Saul's commander-in-chief and although after Gilboa, Ishbaal was technically king of the northern tribes, Abner was the real power behind the throne. In the ancient world one way of staking a claim for power was to sleep with the king's concubine, and when Abner was seen in the bed of Rizpah, Saul's former mistress, Ishbaal saw the writing on the wall. He rebuked Abner weakly but it carried little conviction because he was afraid of him.

Joab and Abner often led their forces against each other, and on one occasion, following bouts of single combat by the pool of Gibeon, Joab's young brother Asahel chased recklessly after the experienced Abner. The older man, not wishing to start a vendetta with Joab's house, rode away trying to dissuade Asahel from the pursuit but he would not be put off and chased relentlessly. The outcome was that Abner thrust backwards with his spear as the young man closed on him, dropping Asahel in his tracks when the spear passed through his body. Incidents such as this exacerbated the ill-feeling which continued for some years as David's forces grew steadily stronger.

Exasperated with Ishbaal, Abner decided to make overtures to David to see if some peaceful solution could be worked out that would draw the two sides together under David. Envoys were sent to test the ground. David replied brusquely by sending a challenge to Ishbaal: 'Hand over to me my wife, Michal, and then we might do business.' The request was granted.

> *Thereupon Ishbosheth [Ishbaal] sent and took her away from her husband, Paltiel son of Laish. Paltiel followed her as far as Bahurim, weeping all the way, until Abner ordered him to go back home, and he went* **(2 Samuel 3:15)**.

Abner then put feelers out in the northern tribes to test the strength of the pro-David lobby and it became clear that there was a strong faction for David in the north. David for his part continued his diplomacy by giving a feast for Abner and his delegation, and the doves of peace fluttered merrily. But these diplomatic moves had been made while Joab was away on a raiding party and when he returned he was furious to learn that David had granted an audience to Abner. Before the northern chief could leave Judah, Joab had him brought back to Hebron where he made an excuse for private conversation in a gateway and treacherously stabbed him to death.

Such was David's lamentation when he heard of Abner's death that one might ask whether perhaps David protested his innocence too much. Be that as it may, Joab kept his command and David's position had been strengthened. It was a position that became totally irresistible when two Benjamite officers, Baanah and Rechab, murdered Ishbaal during his afternoon siesta. David executed the assassins in righteous indignation but he slept that night knowing that at last, at the age of thirty-seven, he was undisputed leader of the whole of Israel.

18 David the King
(c. 1000–961 BC)

2 Samuel 5–10

DAVID, the man of destiny, was anointed king of Judah and Israel in Hebron, following a solemn covenant ceremony before Yahweh. He had the task of uniting a people who fiercely valued their independence and did not always trust the other tribes.

The Philistines had not paid overmuch attention to David when he was king of Judah, but by the time the northern tribes had been added to his domain it was already too late for them to rectify their mistake. The full might of a united Israel was turned against them and though few details of the battles exist, we know that early in David's reign Philistine control of Canaan was utterly broken, leaving them locked in the coastal plain around Gaza. Having subdued the Philistines, he picked off weaker neighbours one by one: Moab, Ammon, Syria, Edom and the Amalekites. Lucrative treaties with others such as Hiram the Phoenician, king of Tyre, left Israel masters of the Promised Land.

With power came change. David now ruled from Dan to Beersheba, and such an empire demanded a suitable capital. Hebron in the south was too remote to be an ideal rallying point for all Israel, so David cast a covetous eye on a well-fortified, independent city-state standing high on a rocky plateau—Jerusalem. It stood 2,550 feet above sea level, thirty-three miles east of the Mediterranean and fourteen miles west of the Dead Sea. It was situated precisely on the border between Judah and the northern tribes and was affiliated to neither. The Jebusites had lived there for years, confident of its impregnable position and sure that they could easily repel invaders. They were wrong. David's troops got inside the city walls by climbing up the water-holes with grappling irons and after that resistance crumbled.

His next move was to make Jerusalem the centre for his religious reforms. Since the early days of Samuel, the Ark had been kept at Kiriath-jearim in the home of Abinadab. David brought it to Jerusalem. Amidst joy and fear (Uzzah's death during the removal was interpreted as a manifestation of Yahweh's wrath that the Ark had been touched), a large procession brought the Ark towards the city, with David leading the way with an uninhibited dance. Michal was disgusted with him.

> *. . . 'What a glorious day for the king of Israel, when he exposed his person in the sight of his servants' slave-girls like any empty-headed fool!'* **(2 Samuel 6:20)**

An 'empty-headed fool' David certainly was not, for what he had made Jerusalem, almost overnight, was 'the city of David' and also Zion, 'the city of God'. Yahweh was once again 'tabernacled' with his people Israel. Some syncretism of religious belief was necessary before Zionism became universally accepted, but it is likely that El Elyon the god of Jerusalem was merged into Yahwehism with the help of Zadok, a priest in Jerusalem and later leader of the priestly office.

Such a large empire could no longer be administered by the charisma of the king alone. A civil service was developed, perhaps on Egyptian lines, and it organised the law, taxation, religious music and festival, military conscription and forced labour. In a single generation the Israelites became prosperous and saw a remarkable rise in their material standard of living. Skilled carpenters, stonemasons and potters flooded into the country from Tyre to build a palace for David and beautify the cities. Traders brought luxury goods to them, unheard of during Saul's more rustic days. But Israel's affluence was bought at a price. Gone was the tribal independence that had long been coveted; allegiance was no longer to the tribal unit but to the king.

The king for his part was Yahweh's sacred and anointed one and the mediator of His divine blessing. He was the unifying figure, the driving force in every sphere of life: religious, political and legal. Israel's power was at its zenith; the king ruled from Lebanon to the Gulf of Aqaba and the border of Egypt. Only one restraining hand prevented him from becoming as tyrannical as contemporary kings, and that hand was with the prophets of Yahweh, fearless men who spoke 'the word of Yahweh' with uncompromising frankness, even when it meant ruffling the feathers of the king.

19 David and Civil War (c. 975 BC)

2 Samuel 11–21

THE early years of David's reign, when 'giddy minds were filled with foreign quarrels', were all success. Then, when the Philistines and surrounding neighbours had been subjugated, Israel should have enjoyed a time of peace and consolidation, but it was not to be. Well-documented court diaries of the time, which largely make up the rich record contained in the books of Samuel, tell a vivid story of intrigue and internal struggle which plagued the king for much of his long reign.

The records show that David, revered though he was by later generations, was not without an Achilles heel which made him very vulnerable. Like other nations' kings, he began to build up a harem, modest at first with just six wives in Hebron, but this was augmented later in Jerusalem when he collected several more wives and concubines. The way in which he procured one such concubine caused such a scandal that even David's popularity waned for a period.

He walked the roof of his palace and saw from there a woman bathing.

The army was away on a mission securing Israel's eastern border at Rabbah against the Ammonites and David was left in Jerusalem. One night, bored and restless, he walked the roof of his palace and saw from there a woman bathing in a house below. She was called Bathsheba and was very beautiful. David's passion, never deep beneath the surface, began to burn. She was the wife of Uriah, one of his soldiers faithfully serving him at Rabbah, but that did not deter David. She was summoned to the palace and seduced, even though she was only just recovering from a period and therefore ritually unclean. Unfortunately for David, this hole-in-the-corner seduction was destined for the front page of the tabloids because she became pregnant. Worried, the king called Uriah home and offered his soldier the privilege of extended leave and, winking lecherously, suggested that his wife might be glad of his company in bed. Uriah refused the offer, saying that he had made a vow that he would forsake such pleasure until the mission was accomplished and all troops could come home together.

> *. . . 'Israel and Judah are under canvas, and so is the Ark, and my lord Joab and your majesty's officers are camping in the open; how can I go home to eat and drink and to sleep with my wife?'*
> **(2 Samuel 11:11)**

David laced Uriah's drinks, but even a drunken Uriah would only sleep with the king's servants. There was one expedient left: Uriah had to die. Sending a letter to Joab by Uriah's own hand, it was fixed that this brave soldier should be exposed in the front line of the battle and left to die. Joab, the ever-faithful commander, fulfilled David's instructions to the letter. After a few crocodile tears from the king, Bathsheba was added to David's harem.

A second, and in the end more damaging, sexual scandal soon broke. David's eldest son Amnon was besotted with his half-sister Tamar who was a young virgin. He mooned around all day unable to get the girl out of his mind. Then, with the help of a cousin he manoeuvred her into his bedroom and brutally raped her. The aftermath was predictable in that 'she bears the load of lust he left behind' and he 'hates himself for his offence'. What was not so predictable was the political storm it was to blow up. The rape became public, but Amnon was David's eldest son and so David did nothing. Desolate, Tamar stayed in the home of her brother Absalom and though he kept calm and quiet, every day her presence fed his hatred of Amnon.

Two years later Absalom threw a sheep-shearers' party in Ephraim. David was invited but did not attend; the princes of Israel, however, including Amnon, did. When the party was in full swing and the guests were well inebriated, Absalom instructed his servants to bide their time, and when Amnon was drunk to kill him. After the murder the disarray was such that a message reached David that all the princes had been killed by Absalom. It was untrue, but nevertheless Absalom thought it prudent to stay in the northern part of the kingdom for the foreseeable future.

It is likely that it was during this separation that Absalom began to think of usurping his father's throne. He was a well-set-up youth, handsome and with a certain charm that attracted many. Away from Jerusalem he was not slow to pick up the vibrations of dissent against the monarchy that existed around Lake Galilee. Joab succeeded in getting Absalom reinstated at Jerusalem after three years, but by then the seeds had gone in deep and in any case he was forbidden access to the palace for a further two years. Headstrong and frustrated at being on the periphery of things, Absalom decided to 'make things happen' and he burnt down Joab's field of barley which was next to his own. It was a plea for recognition, and after five years of separation David relented and re-admitted his wayward son into the palace. It was the king's greatest blunder. Once inside the palace, Absalom flexed his muscles, and provided himself with horses and chariots and an escort of fifty men. Deliberately he sought popularity at the expense of his father, and whenever he came across a man with a grievance he worked on it in such a way that it festered and grew into increasing bitterness towards the king.

After four further years of preparation, Absalom was ready to make a bid for the throne. Hebron had been David's original capital city and people still lived there who resented David's move to Jerusalem. It was here that Absalom, on the pretext of a pilgrimage to Yahweh, blew the trumpet of revolt. Messengers were sent throughout the northern tribes of Israel and the conspiracy gathered strength and was even joined by David's chief councillor, Ahithophel. In this explosive situation the king decided to leave Jerusalem and quickly cross the Jordan in order to assess the numbers of those still faithful to him. Old tribal splits began to gape wide. Meribaal (Mephibosheth), Jonathan's lame son and last royal member from Saul's line, did not follow David but remained in Jerusalem, hoping that after the turmoil and blood-letting the kingdom might return to Saul's line. Shimei, another descendant of Saul, threw stones at the king and cursed him.

'Get out, get out, you scoundrel! you man of blood! Yahweh has taken vengeance on you for the blood of the house of Saul whose throne you stole . . . You murderer, see how your crimes have overtaken you!' **(2 Samuel 16:7-8)**

David was dispirited at the revolt of Absalom, but he was not apathetic and did not leave Jerusalem without a counterplot. The priests Zadok and Abiathar were sent back to Jerusalem with the Ark, along with Hushai, a king's adviser. Ten concubines (later confined to the palace by David because they had been defiled by Absalom) were left behind, and together this group formed an espionage network that would relay information back to David. It worked perfectly. Ahithophel's plans were frustrated so thoroughly by Hushai that he committed suicide. The leakage of information was channelled steadily to the king. Soon army divisions led by Joab, Abishai and Ittai, a faithful mercenary, were ready to begin an offensive against Absalom. By common consent David was not to take part in the hostilities. The battle was joined in the forest of Ephraim but spread out over the whole countryside. It went decisively in David's favour and thousands of Absalom's men fell in a single day. Absalom himself sought refuge in a tree but was spotted by David's men. There was great reluctance to kill him because the king had commanded specifically that his life should be spared, but Joab was a law unto himself and drove three stakes into his chest and killed him. One of the most pitiful pictures painted in the Old Testament is of the king being informed of victory and of Absalom's death.

The king was deeply moved and went up to the roof-chamber over the gate and wept, crying out as he went, 'O, my son! Absalom, my son, my son Absalom! If only I had died instead of you! O Absalom, my son, my son.' **(2 Samuel 18:33)**

So distressed was David that he neglected to thank those who had fought to get the king back to Jerusalem and Joab, once again, was the one to remonstrate with him for this negligence.

Even after Absalom's revolt was crushed, civil unrest continued when northern tribes followed a Benjamite called Sheba who cried:

What share have we in David?
We have no lot in the son of Jesse.
Away to your homes, O Israel **(2 Samuel 20:1)**.

For a time this revolt threatened to be more serious even than Absalom's, but it was finally snuffed out at Abel-beth-maashah in the north of the empire in what is now Lebanon. Sheba's head was thrown over the city wall to placate the avenging fury of Joab.

The superb 'warts and all' portrait of David in the books of Samuel does not gloss over the shortcomings of the king of Israel who was supposed to be 'a man after God's own heart'. Neither are the deep rifts within the empire disguised. That David healed over these rifts for long periods speaks much for his own personality and acumen. The question that was uppermost in people's minds, as David moved into his twilight years, was, 'Could the unity of Israel be maintained without the personal charisma of David the king?' It was a question that would not be answered finally for another forty years.

20 *Nathan and Israel's Prophets* (c. 980–950 BC)

2 Samuel 7; 12:1-25; 1 Kings 1:8-53; 1 Chronicles 29:29

THE reigns of Saul, David and Solomon changed the fabric of Israel's life. Not only had the semi-nomadic people turned into a complex agricultural community, they had also seen a great reduction in their personal freedom. Prescient people feared that to give Israel a king 'like all the other nations' might also introduce the tyranny endured by the other nations. They were right to be fearful. Complete totalitarianism was only avoided because of Israel's *nabi*. This Hebrew word is usually translated as 'prophet', but the *nabi* were not foretellers of the future or clairvoyants so much as people who pierced through the outer shell of national life to check the moral pulse. Their influence on the nation's life was considerable, especially when old ideas of divining the future through dreams and the sacred dice of Urim and Thummin (the ancient equivalent of tossing heads or tails) lost some credibility.

The origins of the *nabi* are obscure. The word was used to describe Moses' brother and spokesman, Aaron, but they are unlikely to have been unique to Israel. Egypt and Canaan had religious men who lived in groups around sacred shrines and hilly cairns associated with worship and sacrifice. Using music, incantation and perhaps drugs, they worked themselves into ecstatic frenzies until the spirit of the gods flooded them. King Saul joined one such Israelite group for a period and claimed that Yahweh's spirit (*ruach* it was called) had invaded him and brought on an ecstatic experience.

> *When they reached the Hill there was a company of prophets coming to meet him, and the spirit of God suddenly took possession of him, so that he too was filled with prophetic rapture. When people who had known him previously saw that he was rapt like the prophets, they said to one another, 'What can have happened to the son of Kish? Is Saul also among the prophets?'* **(1 Samuel 10:10-11)**

The influence of these ***nabi*** grew strong during the reigns of Saul, David and Solomon and it was expedient for the kings to control their activity. This was done by employing them in the cultic practices of the empire, making them part of the establishment and paying them a wage. Some managed to keep their integrity but many 'professional' ***nabi*** tended to trim the words of Yahweh to what the king wanted to hear. Others shunned the royal court altogether and worked in uncontaminated isolation.

Nathan was a ***nabi*** in David's court and his prestige was so high that even the king deferred to him. Shortly after the king's seduction of Bathsheba and the murder of Uriah, it was Nathan who took responsibility for reproaching the king. The way he did it indicates his moral integrity and the subtle cunning the ***nabi*** employed to get their message beneath a man's guard.

> *Yahweh sent Nathan the prophet to David, and when he entered his presence, he said to him, 'There were once two men in the same city, one rich and the other poor. The rich man had large flocks and herds, but the poor man had nothing of his own except one little ewe lamb. He reared it himself and it grew up in his home with his own sons. It ate from his dish, drank from his cup and nestled in his arms; it was like a daughter to him. One day a traveller came to the rich man's house, and he, too mean to take something from his own flocks and herds to serve to his guest, took the poor man's lamb and served up that.' David was very angry, and burst out, 'As Yahweh lives, the man who did this deserves to die! He shall pay for the lamb four times over, because he has done this and shown no pity.' Then Nathan said to David, 'You are the man . . . You have struck down Uriah the Hittite . . . and you have stolen his wife.'* **(2 Samuel 12:1-9)**

The esteem of Nathan was such that he could tell the king not to build a temple for Yahweh in Jerusalem and the king heeded his advice. In the political struggle for succession to David's throne, Nathan threw his weight behind Solomon and probably tipped the balance against Adonijah. There were no areas of life labelled 'religious', 'secular' or 'political' in Nathan's day, and he saw it as his divinely appointed task to speak for Yahweh in every sphere of life. There was no earthly reason why Nathan the ***nabi*** should not be also Nathan the kingmaker. In later generations Israel's ***nabi*** saw it as their duty not only to make kings but to break them as well.

21 Solomon (c. 961–922 BC)

I Kings 1–8:1-21; 9:10–10

DAVID'S last years were times of unrest. Israel was visited by plague and famine and there was great uncertainty about which of David's sons would be the next king. The senile king was tended by a beautiful young girl called Abishag, but even she was unable to stir the old man's passion. Two rival factions supporting Adonijah, the eldest remaining son, and Solomon, a young pretender, each connived to get the official blessing of the ailing David. Adonijah was the obvious choice but he had been spoiled like Amnon and Absalom before him and his boastful and arrogant nature begat enemies. His ambitions were supported by the war veteran Joab and Abiathar the priest. So confident was he of ascending to the throne that he actually threw a coronation party, but he reckoned without the scheming of Bathsheba on her son Solomon's behalf. In one of the king's short bursts of clarity she and Nathan the prophet put her son's case so artfully that the support and blessing of David for Solomon's succession were achieved. Zadok the priest and Benaiah, the captain of David's bodyguard, joined Nathan in a powerful alliance which brought about a successful *coup d'état* when David finally died.

For some time Solomon sat precariously on his throne. Adonijah had not given up his ambitions for the purple and when he sought to marry David's last concubine, Abishag, Solomon was quick to interpret this as a threat to himself and Adonijah was summarily assassinated. This was the beginning of a purge. Joab, David's long-serving commander, saw which way the wind was blowing and pathetically sought refuge at the altar in Yahweh's tent. But there was no refuge. Benaiah, wielding the power that Joab had once enjoyed, struck him down mercilessly. Any remaining threat from Saul's eclipsed descendants was removed when Benaiah killed Shimei, the man who had cursed David during Absalom's rebellion. Abiathar the priest was dismissed from office and sent farming, leaving all priestly duties to Zadok and his family. It was a bloody purge which revived all the old tribal fears about a tyrannical monarchy, but it confirmed Solomon's royal power and left him free to embark on an ambitious programme of expansion—breathtaking in its concept and mind-blowing for a people who, only two generations previously, had been used to rustic living.

Almost overnight the Israelites saw prosperity around them and luxury among the upper classes. Along with fattened fowl, roebucks, gazelles and plentiful wheat, imports flooded into the country as the king increased trade relations and started vast building programmes.

> *The people of Judah and Israel were countless as the sands of the sea; they ate and they drank, and enjoyed life. Solomon ruled over all the kingdoms from the river Euphrates to Philistia and as far as the frontier of Egypt . . .* **(1 Kings 4:20-21)**

Jerusalem was a hive of industry and enterprise, and in a twenty-year building boom a royal palace, a temple, stables, fortifications, courthouses, a house for Pharaoh's daughter (whom Solomon had married in an alliance with Egypt) and an enormous harem rose from the dust in a magnificent display of opulence. Hiram, a master craftsman from Tyre, was employed to supervise building and only the best materials were used. Gold adorned everything because silver 'was reckoned of no value in the days of Solomon'. Cedars and pines were transported by sea down the Mediterranean coast from Lebanon and huge stones were skilfully faced and built into impressive colonnades. His palace was magnificent, but the temple the most important. It took seven years to build, and though modestly sized by the standards of Christian cathedrals,

Jerusalem was a hive of industry and enterprise.

it was a remarkable architectural achievement. Its Phoenician style made it difficult for traditional Israelites to accept, but it had a special windowless room at its heart which housed the Ark, and therefore the temple was seen as the permanent house of Yahweh replacing the Tent of Meeting which had been the focus of Yahwehism since the Exodus from Egypt. The Ark was carefully placed under the golden wings of two fifteen-foot cherubim and the windowless room, lined with cedar, became Yahweh's throne room, the Holy of Holies.

Away from Jerusalem, Solomon built chariot cities and fortification on strategic trade routes such as those at Gezer and Megiddo. Large-scale excavations at Megiddo have revealed evidence of stalls for at least 450 horses. His commercial enterprises included merchant shipping deals which extended his influence to the Indian Ocean and the Red Sea, horse trading on a grand scale and industrial plant on the Gulf of Aqaba where the smelting and refining of copper and iron took place, making it the 'Pittsburgh of Palestine'. Solomon's empire was a wonder of the ancient world and brought him into the same orbit as the legendary Queen of Sheba.

How was all this achieved? Sadly, along with the growing opulence went a ruthless centralisation of power and a large bureaucracy, completely alien to Israel's traditions. Old tribal boundaries were deliberately replaced by tax districts, some of them supervised by Solomon's own family. Israelites were conscripted into national service to make sure that the great cedars of Lebanon were felled and transported to Jerusalem. Hundreds of thousands were employed in labour camps and compelled to live oppressed lives in their own land. The king's superb buildings were raised on the blood of Israel's peasants.

Solomon's name has been handed onto posterity as the epitome of wisdom, and the wise sayings in the Old Testament book of Proverbs were dedicated to him. But it was a superficial wisdom. What Solomon failed to understand was that the dreams and traditions of his people were stronger than the glittering empire he had erected on the foundation of David. Even at the pinnacle of his achievement, rebellion was burrowing into the structure of his empire like termites into an oak. Soon the whole splendid edifice would come crashing to the ground.

22 Rehoboam and Jeroboam I *(922–901 BC)*

I Kings 11:26–12; 14

BY brute force and tyranny Solomon had managed to keep most of David's empire intact. He had increased the sophistication and material wealth of the nation, but he had not won the affection of the people as his father had done. The tenuous unity between Judah and the northern tribes showed signs of fracturing and intrigue was rife.

Solomon had promoted an energetic young man called Jeroboam to be charge hand of the labour gangs in the north, and Jeroboam quickly sensed the anger felt by the northerners at the king's regime. The anger was fuelled by a *nabi* called Ahijah who complained that simple Yahwehism was being corrupted by the king's tolerance of other religions, which diluted and enfeebled the nation's spiritual life. In a typically dramatic act, which was a promise for the future rather than a mere gesture, Ahijah stopped Jeroboam on a deserted stretch of road coming north from Jerusalem and symbolically ripped up a new tunic he was wearing. He ripped it into twelve pieces and gave ten of them to Jeroboam to signify that Yahweh was about to give the northern tribes of Israel to him. The die had been cast, and though Jeroboam had to seek refuge with King Shishak of Egypt, to escape the clutches of the suspicious Solomon he waited in exile like a shadowy Lenin for his moment to arrive.

The moment came with the king's death. Rehoboam seemed to be the unchallenged successor, and representatives from the tribal areas gathered at the ancient site of Shechem to declare their allegiance to the new king. Before the declaration, however, they wanted some assurance that Rehoboam would reduce taxes, abolish conscription and lessen Israel's bureaucracy. Jeroboam led an assembly to petition Rehoboam:

> *. . . 'Your father laid a cruel yoke upon us; but if you will now lighten the cruel slavery he imposed on us and the heavy yoke he laid on us, we will serve you.'* **(1 Kings 12:4)**

Pig-headedly, Rehoboam refused advice offered him by his elder statesmen and listened instead to his younger cronies. After three days he gave the assembly his reply:

> *'. . . "My little finger is thicker than my father's loins. My father laid a heavy yoke on you; I will make it heavier. My father used the whip on you; but I will use the lash."'* **(1 Kings 12:10-11)**

This was too much for the northerners to stomach. As one man they cried:

> *What share have we in David?*
>
> . . .
>
> *Away to your homes, O Israel;*
> *now see to your own house, David* **(1 Kings 12:16)**.

Jeroboam raised the banner of revolt and the northern tribes united under his leadership. Rehoboam re-asserted himself and sent Adoram the commander of forced levies to whip the rebels back into line, but he was stoned to death. Rehoboam beat an undignified retreat to Jerusalem where he briefly toyed with the idea of resisting the insurrection, but he thought better of it. Jeroboam was declared the first king of the new independent state of Israel and Rehoboam was left to carry on David's line in the smaller kingdom of Judah. The kingdom of David had been divided and it was never to be rejoined.

Jeroboam's immediate problem was to bring a sense of unity to Israel and an administrative structure that bred confidence and stability. He fortified Shechem and made it his capital city. He made Bethel in the south, and Dan in the north, religious sanctuaries to replace Jerusalem. At these sanctuaries he set up bulls and replaced the old Levitic priesthood with a new priestly order. Their allegiance was still to Yahweh, but bulls savoured too much of Canaanite fertility religion and they were regarded with total abhorrence by later Deuteronomic editors. They castigated Jeroboam for setting up these sanctuaries in opposition to Jerusalem and blamed him for the religious apostasy of later generations.

When reading Jeroboam's 'bad press', we have to bear in mind that we are reading the biased accounts of religious reformers from the southern state of Judah. To get a more balanced picture we should remember that Jeroboam reigned for twenty-one years and established the northern tribes as a kingdom in their own right, whereas Rehoboam, in Judah, reigned a mere seven years, during which time Jerusalem was attacked by Egypt and the splendid temple of Solomon was severely plundered. All the gold shields, which adorned the walls, had to be replaced by bronze replicas.

The brief heady days of great power had gone from Israel, never to return. But the collective memory of the nation never forgot the glory that had once been theirs under David, and they yearned for a second David who one day would return to restore Israel's former glories.

23 Toil and Trouble
(900–876 BC)

1 Kings 15–16:22

THE break-up of Solomon's empire created a power vacuum in the Middle East which neither Israel nor Judah were equipped to fill. Egypt woke up from the lethargy that had paralysed her since the days of Moses, and King Shishak successfully attacked Jerusalem and ransacked the temple. Inscriptions found on the magnificent temple of Karnak, near Luxor, show that even though Shishak was unable to achieve a lasting conquest, many other Judean and Israelite cities fell to him at this time.

Judah, oppressed by the stronger Israel, formed an alliance with Israel's northern neighbour Syria. In the short term, it was a good political move because it forced Israel to take military precautions to safeguard her northern border and thereby relieved the pressure on Judah. In the long term, however, it was an ominous decision which presaged the beginning of the end of independence for both Israel and Judah. It was an unhappy time for the Hebrew kingdoms, who, within a generation had slipped into the second division of political power. Judah kept faith with the offspring of David and kept his descendants on the throne. Not all were capable kings, but the faithfulness to David's line provided Judah with a continuity that Israel never managed to achieve.

In the north, Jeroboam reigned for twenty-one years and established Israel as an independent kingdom, but his son Nadab lasted only two years before his throne was usurped by a soldier from the tribe of Issachar called Baasha. After his *coup d'état* all Jeroboam's male offspring were slaughtered in a blood bath, which became a dismal feature of Israel's history. Baasha set up his throne at Tirzah and reigned for twenty-four years but, as with Jeroboam, once he was dead bloody anarchy followed. Baasha's son Elah was treacherously killed by Zimri, a leader of the chariot forces. All Baasha's male offspring were killed.

... he struck down all the family of Baasha and left not a single mother's son alive, kinsman or friend **(1 Kings 16:11)**.

If Zimri expected Israel to rally to his side he was mistaken. The army's allegiance did not swing to him but to another military commander called Omri, and he immediately besieged Tirzah. Zimri had badly miscalculated his hand and he

... retreated to the keep of the royal palace, set the whole of it on fire over his head and so perished
(1 Kings 16:18).

He had reigned for one week!

The religious life of the Hebrews suffered during these turbulent years. A prophet of Yahweh called Jehu did denounce Baasha for his lack of religious zeal, but by and large it was a period of religious and moral laxity. In Israel the strict moral code of Yahweh was watered down to accommodate Canaanite fertility cults, while in the south Solomon's Ammonite queen had introduced practices that were having a disastrous effect on Judah's religion. Sacred shrines sprang up on 'every high hill' and 'under every green tree' and these shrines encouraged sacred prostitutes, many of whom were male.

Zimri set the palace on fire over his head and so perished.

... all over the country there were male prostitutes attached to the shrines, and the people adopted all the abominable practices of the nations whom Yahweh had dispossessed in favour of Israel
(1 Kings 14:24).

Asa, Rehoboam's grandson, did attempt religious reforms, and went so far as to destroy an obscene object erected by the queen mother for the worship of the Canaanite goddess Asherah, but the general drift in north and south was towards moral laxity.

Yahwehism had lost its crusading zeal and was in danger of being buried under resurgent Canaanite gods. If the religion of Moses was to survive in the midst of such moral turpitude, Yahweh desperately needed a champion.

24 Omri *(876–869 BC)*

1 Kings 16:23-28

THE book of Kings devotes only six verses to describing the life and times of Omri, one of the northern kingdom's most formidable kings, a man who earned the title 'David of the north'. The reason for this is that the Deuteronomic historian who chose the material for his 'history' saw nothing of religious importance in Omri's reign, apart from his negligence in not destroying the high places associated with Canaanite religion. That single fact was enough to label Omri 'a bad king' in the editor's eyes. Fortunately, there is evidence other than that in the Bible that shows beyond doubt that Omri achieved a great deal once he had seen off the threat of a military rival called Tibni and established himself on the throne of Israel.

One of his first actions as king was to buy a hill from a man called Shemer and build on it the great city of Samaria, which became his royal capital. It is the only example of an Israelite city not built on a previous foundation, and its splendour has only been discovered by modern archaeological excavation. Trade relations with Phoenicia, which had been a feature of life under David and Solomon, were revived under Omri, and the impressive buildings of Samaria bear witness to the marvellous skills of the artisans of Tyre. Discoveries made on the site of old Samaria include some of the finest ever found by Middle Eastern archaeology. It used to be thought that the scorn of the prophet Amos for Israel's 'houses of ivory' was exaggeration, but the twentieth-century findings have revealed, beyond any shadow of doubt, that Omri's palaces were as opulent as Amos suggests.

Commerce prospered as the king formed lucrative alliances with surrounding nations, and particularly with the Phoenicians. To cement one such alliance, Crown Prince Ahab was joined by marriage to Princess Jezebel of Tyre, a union that had grave repercussions for Israel. Under Omri's vigorous leadership, Israel's borders were secured, and territory that had been in dispute since the days of Solomon was possessed by Israel. The Moabite Stone, a black basalt stele, four feet high, inscribed by Mesha, the king of Moab, makes it clear that Moab was subject to Omri during his reign. Generations after his death and the slaughter of his offspring, the Assyrian records still referred to Israel as 'the land of Omri'.

However, not everyone welcomed the return of the good times to Israel. The material prosperity tended to be enjoyed in the cities at the expense of the country folk who were faced with harsh taxation and usurious interest rates. Some had never had it so good; others felt oppressed. Moreover, the Hebrew idea of the inviolability of hereditary property, so precious to a people whose roots went back to slavery, was threatened with the increased power of the king. At the time, the great moral principles of Yahwehism were being eroded by the growing influence of Canaanite religions supported by Jezebel. The God of Israel was swamped in the surge of materialism and the accompanying revival of fertility religion.

The battle for the spirit of Israel came to a dramatic climax during the reign of Omri's son, Ahab. Yahweh's champion moved from the wings to centre stage, and his name was Elijah!

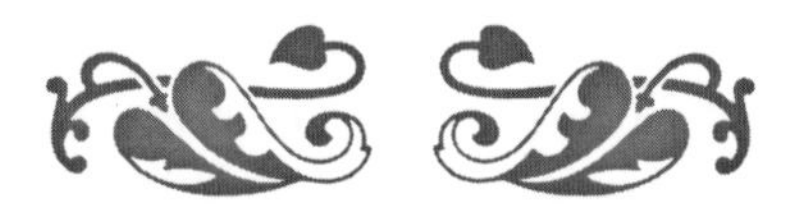

25 Ahab and Jezebel (869–850 BC)

1 Kings 16:29-34; 20; 22; 2 Kings 9:30–10:17

SEEN from a political perspective, the reign of Ahab and his queen Jezebel was not without achievement or merit. Their marriage had been part of Omri's alliance with Phoenicia, and the alliance had been beneficial to Israel's prosperity and security. It provided Israel with an ally at a time when the Syrian Benhadad was acting in a bellicose manner and threatening to over-run the country. In two successive campaigns, Ahab humiliated the Syrian king, and after an overwhelming victory at Aphek had him captive. Ahab spared Benhadad's life and earned a stern rebuke from the traditional Yahwehists who were demanding that he should be slaughtered according to *cherem*, the rules of holy war. However, non-biblical evidence suggests that Ahab could have had shrewd military reasons for sparing Benhadad's life.

To the north, the giant kingdom of Assyria was beginning to flex her muscles and looked with covetous eyes towards the Mediterranean end of the Middle East's fertile crescent. If smaller kingdoms were to resist the Assyrian juggernaut, they could do it only by combining their armies. The Assyrian king, Shalmaneser III, moved south and engaged these allied armies at a place called Qarqar, north of Damascus. The Bible has no record of this battle, but Shalmaneser's annals explain in some detail that the battle did take place (probably in 853 BC) and that Ahab contributed 10,000 foot soldiers and 2,000 chariots, by far the largest contribution to the allied forces. The Assyrian claimed a great victory, after the manner of war communiqués, but this can be taken with a pinch of salt because he gave up his expansive ideas and withdrew his troops, presumably to tend a bloody nose.

This temporary withdrawal left Israel and Syria free to renew their more parochial squabbles, and Ahab felt strong enough to lay claim to Rammoth-gilead, a border town where ownership had been a matter of dispute for some years (rather like Berwick between the Scots and the English). Ahab succeeded in co-opting the help of Jehoshaphat, the king of Judah, who seems to have been dragged into the dispute as a weak, subservient neighbour. The auguries for success were good. Professional prophets fell over themselves to assure the king that victory was certain, the only dissenting voice being a courageous Yahwehist called Micaiah, who declared:

> *... 'I will say only what Yahweh tells me to say ... I saw all Israel scattered on the mountains, like sheep without a shepherd ...'* **(1 Kings 22:14-17)**

He was beaten up and locked away lest he should undermine national confidence. A worried Ahab decided to keep a low profile during the battle, no doubt bearing Micaiah's words in mind, but he could not hold off the hand of fate.

> *... one man drew his bow at random and hit the king of Israel where the breastplate joins the plates of the armour. So he [Ahab] said to his driver, 'Wheel round and take me out of the line; I am wounded.' When the day's fighting reached its height, the king was facing the Aramaeans propped up in his chariot, and the blood from his wound flowed down upon the floor of the chariot; and in the evening he died* **(1 Kings 22:34-35).**

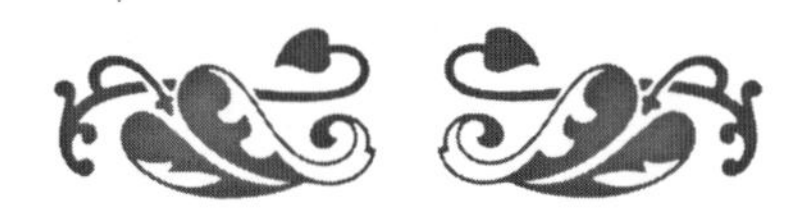

26 Elijah (869–842 BC)

1 Kings 17–19; 21; 2 Kings 1–2:18

AGAINST this political backdrop, a religious struggle was taking place for the soul of Israel. The queen Jezebel was not prepared to be simply a decoration for her husband. She was a passionately evangelical Baal worshipper who insisted on freedom of worship for herself and coerced many others into Baal worship as well. Ahab was swept up in her religious fervour and hundreds of Yahwehists were massacred. Obadiah, the chief steward in the royal house, remained faithful and saved a hundred prophets by hiding them in caves and smuggling food to them, but they were bleak days for those who sought to hang on to the traditional faith in the God of Moses.

At this harrowing time, made worse by a prolonged famine, a mysterious *nabi* called Elijah kept himself alive in the desert by moving steadily eastwards looking for water supplies. Legends sprang up about his great spiritual powers and stories were passed on that even claimed that he could raise people from the dead. When the famine was reaching its height in Samaria, Elijah moved out of the desert to spearhead the resistance to Jezebel. Fearlessly he faced the king.

> *As soon as Ahab saw Elijah, he said to him, 'Is it you, you troubler of Israel?' 'It is not I who have troubled Israel,' he replied, 'but you and your father's family, by forsaking the commandments of Yahweh and following Baal.'* **(1 Kings 18:17-18)**

Elijah's message was that the time had come to choose who was the true God of Israel. For too long the nation had 'sat on the fence'; now Israel had to decide. With great relish the narrative tells the story of the confrontation on Mount Carmel. An altar was set up, complete with a sacrificial bull, and the hundreds of Baal's prophets were invited by Elijah to invoke their god to send fire and consume the offering. They danced around the altar, crying out to Baal, but the offering remained. They gashed themselves with swords and from morning to late afternoon they raved and ranted in a desperate bid to stir Baal from the sleep Elijah said he was taking. It was to no avail—the offering remained.

Then Elijah prayed to Yahweh and

> *. . . the fire of Yahweh fell. It consumed the whole-offering, the wood, the stones, and the earth, and licked up the water in the trench. When all the people saw it, they fell prostrate and cried, 'Yahweh is God, Yahweh is God.' Then Elijah said to them, 'Seize the prophets of Baal; let not one of them escape.' They seized them, and Elijah took them down to the Kishon and slaughtered them there in the valley* **(1 Kings 18:38-40)**.

On the face of it, Yahweh had been vindicated and Elijah had won the day, but the truth is more complicated than legend would suggest. Another story gives a highly significant account of Elijah fleeing for his life from Queen Jezebel. So fearful is he that he travels far into the south, through Judah, the Negeb and into the Sinai peninsula almost to the shores of the Red Sea. In short, he returns to the origins of Israel's faith, to the sacred mountain of Sinai, where Yahweh had first revealed himself to Moses. It was a pilgrimage taken to bolster a dwindling faith, and on that mountain the central truth of Yahwehism, the very foundation of Moses' own belief, comes to Elijah like a slap in the face. Yahweh is not a nature god, tied to a land; He is the force behind everything, and most important of all He is the God who is involved in the affairs of men, the God who is known by the things he does. So what was Elijah doing on a mountain, hidden away from the hurly-burly of life? Yahweh was the Lord of history and commanding him to return to the activity of the political arena.

Elijah is obedient to the command, and leaving behind the mystic contemplation of his mountain retreat he returns to Samaria. Here he discovers the latest of Jezebel's infamies. A man called Naboth owned a vineyard next to a plot of land belonging to the king, and the king wanted it. Naboth, according to ancient custom, was not prepared to sell land that had belonged to his fathers because it was sacred to him. Ahab was annoyed, but there did not seem to be much he could do about it. Jezebel, however, did not have the scruples of her husband.

'Are you or are you not king in Israel?' she asked (1 Kings 21:7). Then, taking matters into her own hand, she dreamed up spurious charges of treason and blasphemy against Naboth who, on the strength of these charges, was stoned to death without trial or the chance to defend himself. Ahab was free to take over Naboth's land, but when he moved to take the vineyard he was met by Elijah who denounced the king.

> *'. . . "Have you killed your man, and taken his land as well?" Say to him, "This is the word of Yahweh: Where dogs licked the blood of Naboth, there dogs shall lick your blood."' Ahab said to Elijah, 'Have you found me, my enemy?' 'I have found you', he said, 'because you have sold yourself to do what is wrong in the eyes of Yahweh. I will sweep you away and destroy every mother's son of the house of Ahab in Israel . . . I will deal with your house as I did with the house of Jeroboam . . .' When Ahab heard this, he rent his clothes, put on sackcloth and fasted; he lay down in his sackcloth and went about muttering to himself* **(1 Kings 21:19-27)**.

Elijah had re-stated the claims of Yahweh for the allegiance of his people, and though his feud with Jezebel and Ahab's son continued for some years, the message of Elijah the Tishbite was never forgotten. Legend has him whisked away to heaven in a whirlwind with his disciple Elisha crying after him:

> *'My father, my father, the chariots and the horsemen of Israel!'* **(2 Kings 2:12)**

It was a worthy tribute to a man who proved that truth, spoken without equivocation, can be more powerful than arms and armies. Israel never forgot Elijah the prophet who, in time, was revered almost as much as Moses. Indeed, the belief grew in some circles that one day Elijah would return and his return would usher in the glorious day when Yahweh would reign supreme and all men bow their knees to him.

27 Elisha and Jehu's Revolution *(842–815 BC)*

2 Kings 2:19–10; 13:14-20

AHAB was succeeded on the throne by his son Ahaziah, but early in his reign he fell through the latticed window of his roof chamber and died shortly afterwards. He was replaced by his brother Jehoram and it was during his reign that Mesha the king of Moab tried to throw off the imperialism of Israel. Since Omri's day they had been forced to hand over to Israel quotas of wool from the high-quality sheep that grazed on their land. On Ahab's death these quotas were withheld and Jehoram marched against Mesha, accompanied by Jehoshaphat of Judah and the king of Edom. They seemed to be winning the day until Mesha, in desperation, sacrificed his son and crown prince to the Moabite god Chemosh. The sacrifice was performed on the city wall in full view of the allied Israeli armies and caused such consternation among the troops that they immediately forsook their posts and went home. The Moabite Stone, discovered in 1868, makes the extravagant claim that Israel was destroyed forever in this battle.

Relations between Israel and Judah were cordial at this time, and marriages were arranged between the two royal houses. Most of the information for this period indicates that great friction existed between Israel and Syria (Aram) and the folk tales about Elijah's successor Elisha are woven into this conflict. They are romantic stories about Elisha's ability to make an axehead float, turn puddles into blood, feed a hundred folk with a few loaves and bring the dead back to life. In one such story, Elisha causes two bears to maul forty-two small boys because they called him 'bald head'! More interestingly, the stories show Elisha as just one—probably the leader—of a band of prophets, banded together to serve Yahweh, whose influence spread beyond Israel and Judah to Syria as well. That seems to be the point in the tale of Naaman, the Syrian commander, who was cured of his leprosy by obeying Elisha's command to bathe in the River Jordan. So grateful is Naaman that he takes a couple of loads of earth back to Syria so that he can worship Yahweh there!

The king of Syria at this time was Benhadad and he was determined to defeat Israel once and for all. He called up his entire army and besieged Samaria. The siege lasted months and people inside the city were desperate for food. People starved; others resorted to cannibalism, and a donkey's head was sold for an exorbitant eighty pieces of silver. Jehoram, beside himself with anguish, looked round for a scapegoat and tried to pin the blame for Samaria's plight on Elisha, who had been advocating that if faith in Yahweh was kept all would be well.

> *'Look at our plight! [cried the king] This is Yahweh's doing. Why should I wait any longer for him to help us?'* **(2 Kings 6:33)**

Elisha's confidence did not waver.

> *'By this time tomorrow a shekel will buy a measure of flour or two measures of barley, in the gateway of Samaria.'* **(2 Kings 7:1)**

At twilight that evening, four lepers, desperate for food, crept into the Syrian camp and were staggered to find it deserted. Everything had been abandoned—tents, horses, asses, food, drink, clothes, silver and gold had all been left in a frenzied rush to leave the site. When the lepers shouted the news to guards in Samaria, people pushed open the gates and plundered the camp. The following day food was dirt cheap and Samaria's life returned to normal. What caused the Syrians to break camp in such haste? Some claimed that Yahweh had 'caused the Aramaean army to hear a sound like that of chariots and horses and of a great host', but it is just as likely that Benhadad got wind of a plot, instigated by Elisha, to steal his throne, and therefore retreated post haste to Damascus to abort the revolution.

Elisha's influence was at its height and he was ready to shape the destiny of Israel and Syria. It was Elisha who filled Hazael's mind with such 'vaulting ambition' that he was led to smother the ailing Benhadad with a wet towel and claim Syria's throne for himself. Then, when Israel's forces were once again contesting with Syria for Ramoth-gilead, Elisha went into the Israelite camp while Jehoram was away, and anointed Jehu as king, telling him it was his responsibility to purge the nation of Ahab's family and eradicate the pernicious poison of Jezebel and Baal worship.

When Jehu rejoined the king's officers, they said to him, 'Is all well? What did the crazy fellows want with you?' 'You know him and the way his thoughts run', he said. 'Nonsense!' they replied; 'tell us what happened.' 'I will tell you exactly what he said: "This is the word of Yahweh: I anoint you king over Israel."' They snatched up their cloaks and spread them under him on the stones of the steps, and sounded the trumpet and shouted, 'Jehu is king.' **(2 Kings 9:11-13)**

Thus began the bloodiest massacre recorded in the Bible. Jehoram was recuperating from battle injuries in Jezreel, and Ahaziah, the king of Judah, was paying him a 'get well soon' visit. Word came to them that Jehu was heading for Jezreel, driving his chariot at a furious pace. Bewildered, the king rode out to meet his commander to ascertain the reason for the hasty visit. He soon discovered that Jehu was not solicitous for his health. An arrow pierced

Jehu was heading for Jezreel, driving his chariot at a furious pace.

Jehoram's heart and Ahaziah received injuries from which he later died. With didactic irony the king's body was thrown onto the plot of land stolen from Naboth by Ahab and Jezebel.

By this time Jezebel knew what was afoot, and with Cleopatra's style she 'painted her eyes, dressed her hair' and waited by an upstairs window for Jehu's arrival. Then she cried,

> *. . . 'Is it peace, you Zimri, you murderer of your master?'* **(2 Kings 9:31)**

Jehu's response was that she should be thrown from the window and . . .

> *They threw her down, and some of her blood splashed on to the wall and the horses, which trampled her underfoot. Then he [Jehu] went in and ate and drank* (2 Kings 9:33).

With great efficiency the descendants of the Omri/Ahab line, some seventy sons, were rounded up and murdered. Their bodies were decapitated and left outside Jezreel. Other nobles, close friends and priests were added to the holocaust. Relatives of Judah's king, Ahaziah, were unfortunate enough to fall into his hands and they too were slaughtered. Jehonadab, a strict Rechabite, who held tenaciously to Israel's old Yahwehist traditions, joined Jehu at this point to complete the extermination. The prophets of Baal were summoned to attend a sacrifice for Baal-Melkart, and when they were assembled and it was confirmed that no prophet of Yahweh was among them, it was revealed that the prophets themselves were to be the sacrifice. They were cut down, the sacred poles and pillars were burnt and the temple of Baal itself made into a lavatory.

Jehu's revolution was complete. The Omri dynasty had ended in a welter of blood and the cult of Baal had received a devastating blow. In some circles the work of Jehu was acclaimed. The *cherem* had been applied to the letter and the religious crusade of Elijah and Elisha had been vindicated. But not everybody approved of the blood-letting, and years later the prophet Hosea called one of his children 'Jezreel' in memory of those people who died in the horrors of Jehu's revolt.

28 Athaliah and Joash
(842–800 BC)

2 Kings 11–12

JEHU'S revolution in Israel had dreadful repercussions in Judah. His blood lust had included the murder of Ahaziah, the king of Judah, and many of his royal household. This opened a way for Athaliah, the queen mother, to grasp the reigns of power. She added to Jehu's slaughter by assassinating remaining members of the royal family. Great King David's line was in grave danger of extermination; it continued only in the fragile body of Ahaziah's baby son Joash. Realising the awful danger, Jehoida, the chief priest, kidnapped the baby and along with his wife Jehosheba, who was also the baby's aunt, organised a watch to be kept over the child at all times. He was hidden inside the temple precincts, and guards, sworn to secrecy, made sure that unauthorised people were kept away.

These orders were carried out to the letter, and six years later when Joash was seven, Jehoida

> *. . . put the crown on his head, handed him the warrant and anointed him king. The people clapped their hands and shouted, 'Long live the king.'* **(2 Kings 11:12)**

Athaliah rushed to see what the commotion was all about and saw the young king standing on the dais.

> *Then Athaliah rent her clothes and cried, 'Treason! Treason!'* **(2 Kings 11:14)**

Jehosheba organised a watch to be kept over the child at all times.

She was dragged from the temple and put to death publicly by the horse entry to the royal palace. Jehoida then organised a solemn re-dedication ceremony to Yahweh, and in the middle of general celebrations the people pulled down the temple of Baal. It was a priestly revolution which paralleled Jehu's prophetic revolution in the north, though it was to preserve the royal line rather than usurp it and it happened without an accompanying blood bath.

Joash reigned for forty years and spent much of this time refurbishing the temple with money raised from free-will offerings. Workmen were placed on trust and got on with the work without lining their own pockets. Sadly for Joash, the latter years of his reign were disrupted by Hazael the Syrian who threatened Jerusalem and was only bought off by the handing over of temple treasures. The final moment of Joash's reign was tragedy when he was treacherously slain by his servants.

During the reigns of Jehu and Joash, the Assyrians continued to poke threatening fingers into Palestinian affairs. Jehu was one of several rulers who were compelled to pay tribute to Shalmaneser III, who described himself self-effacingly on the famous Black Obelisk as

> *... the mighty king, king of the universe, king without rival, the autocrat, the powerful one of the four regions of the world.*

He exaggerated perhaps, but he also indicated the colossal ambition that did not augur well for the future of Israel.

The Assyrians

THE Assyrian Empire was centred around the great cities of Ashur and Ninevah on the Tigris river. From about 900 BC their population grew rapidly and they sought to expand their boundaries. Their expansion was resisted, and consequently they had to increase their military strength in order to survive. They became a nation constantly on military alert and soon acquired a reputation for cruelty. They were masters of siegecraft and charioteering and used iron weapons, such as swords and arrows, with great skill.

The economy was based on military strength and every man could be called up for military service. Nevertheless, they did not resist culture, and much of our knowledge of the ancient world is due to the discovery of Assyrian libraries which include sections on astronomy, medicine and religion. The national god of the empire was Ashur who was depicted as being as warlike as the Assyrians themselves. Their art was secular rather than religious, and reliefs of defeated soldiers being impaled on stakes give a strong clue as to why the Assyrian armies put the fear of Ashur into weaker peoples.

The military basis of the Assyrian Empire demanded heavy taxation, much of which was imposed on defeated peoples such as the Israelites under Menahem:

> *In his days Pul king of Assyria invaded the country, and Menahem gave him a thousand talents of silver to obtain his help in strengthening his hold upon the kingdom* **(2 Kings 15:19)**.

The great building projects of various Assyrian kings also demanded manpower, and this was provided by captive peoples carted away into exile. From Israel's capital city of Samaria alone, 27,290 men were forced to leave their homeland to swell the labour market. It is possible that some of the bas-reliefs discovered by A.H. Layard between 1845 and 1851, and transported with difficulty to the British Museum in London, could have been the work of forced labourers.

Tiglath-pileser III (known as Pul in 2 Kings) was not the first Assyrian to threaten Israel and Syria in the west, but he was the man who established impressive road systems across the empire to ensure rapid communications with his provincial governors and make an attack southwards inevitable.

29 Right or Wrong in the Eyes of Yahweh

2 Kings 14

THE compilers of the Old Testament books 1 and 2 Kings had before them comprehensive annals of the achievements of the respective kings. Tantalisingly, we are given snippets of information from these annals, but few details:

> *The other acts and events of the reign of Joash are recorded in the annals of the kings of Judah. His servants revolted against him and struck him down in the house of Millo on the descent to Silla* **(2 Kings 12:19-20)**.

> *The other events of Amaziah's reign are recorded in the annals . . . A conspiracy was formed against him in Jerusalem and he fled to Lachish; but they sent after him to Lachish and put him to death there* **(2 Kings 14:18-19)**.

> *The other events of Jeroboam [II]'s reign, and all his achievements, his exploits, the wars he fought and how he recovered Damascus and Hamath in Jaudi for Israel are recorded in the annals of the kings of Israel* **(2 Kings 14:28)**.

The reason for the dearth of information is simple—it did not interest them! The compilers were not concerned with military exploits, but with religious faithfulness. Furthermore, their work was done hundreds of years *after* the events described, and their yardstick was that of a later group of people who were influenced by a religious revolution yet to come. In other words, kings such as Joash, Amaziah and Jeroboam II were being judged by criteria they knew nothing about! All the kings of Israel, and some of the kings of Judah, were denounced, not because they were exceptionally wicked, but because they did not sacrifice to Yahweh at Jerusalem's temple or get rid of the ancient hill shrines. Obviously, Israel's kings could not advocate sacrifice in Jerusalem because it was not their kingdom, and why should they destroy the hill-shrines that had been sacred since time immemorial? If sacrifice was only legitimate in Jerusalem why was Elijah not condemned for his sacrifice on Mount Carmel? This hindsight criticism of Israel's kings can be compared to a twentieth-century historian criticising Oliver Cromwell without understanding the passion that sparked off Britain's own Civil War.

Only seven verses are allocated to Jeroboam II's forty-one-year reign over Israel, even though he re-established the borders and completely subdued Syria. He brought security back to a land that for years had been the playground of soldiers, thugs and pillagers. Things had not been so good since the days of Omri. The shrine at Bethel was packed solid with people who wanted to thank Yahweh for their prosperity. To many, the bulging storehouses and increased luxuries were an indication of divine pleasure and a proof that the 'Day of Yahweh' was imminent.

One man who did not see things this way was an eighth-century shepherd called Amos. One day he arrived at Bethel with a message that made him as welcome as a coffin at a wedding.

30 Amos (750 BC)

Amos 1–4:5; 5:16–6:7; 7–8

AMOS lived and worked as a shepherd in the region of Tekoa in Judah, a high-lying town, not far from the Dead Sea and six miles from Bethlehem. He looked after those peculiar sheep of the area that have short legs and ugly faces but superb wool. In his spare time he cultivated figs.

One day, as he was working, he felt quite clearly that his God, Yahweh, was speaking directly to him. He felt convinced that he had to travel the forty miles or so, past Jerusalem into the land of Israel, and delivery a message to the worshippers swarming round the sanctuary at Bethel. When he arrived, trade was brisk, brewers were doing a roaring trade and posh houses were springing up almost overnight in an orgy of spending. But Amos was quick to see that when you scratched away the veneer of Israel's life there was serious cancer underneath.

With cunning style, Amos chose a convenient spot and began to denounce the sins of Israel's nearest neighbours—people such as the Syrians, Phoenicians, Edomites, Moabites, and even his own people of Judah. He was warmly applauded. Then, like a striking viper, he directed his venom towards the self-satisfied Israelites around him with withering questions (Amos 1–2:8).

—How can Yahweh be pleased with you when in time of plenty the heads of the poor are being ground into the dust?

—How can He be pleased when judges are being bribed and innocent men are being found guilty?

—How can He be pleased when a father and son visit the same temple prostitute?

—How can He be pleased when rich men on their pleasant sub-urban hillsides drink wine by the bowlful and their wives, like fat cows, drive them to greater excesses?

Some of those worshipping could not wait for the sabbath to be over so that they could continue their fraudulent practices—giving short weight, tilting the scales, overcharging, putting dust at the bottom of the bags of wheat, or cheating the destitute for the price of a pair of sandals (Amos 2:6-8; 4:1; 5:7-11).

It was true the temple was full of pious worshippers who prayed incessantly for the 'Day of Yahweh' to come, but they were

> *Fools who long for the day of Yahweh,*
> *what will the day of Yahweh mean to you?*
> *It will be darkness, not light.*
> *It will be as when a man runs from a lion,*
> *and a bear meets him,*
> *or turns into a house and leans his hand on the wall,*
> *and a snake bites him.*
> *The day of Yahweh is indeed darkness, not light.*
> *a day of gloom with no dawn* **(Amos 5:18-20).**

Amos insisted that 'true religion' went beyond ritual to righteousness.

> *Spare me the sound of your songs;*
> *I cannot endure the music of your lutes.*
> *Let justice roll on like a river*
> *and righteousness like an ever-flowing stream'*
> **(Amos 5:23-24)**

Jeroboam would not live forever and the good times would soon be gone. Already darkly gathering in the north like locusts were the hordes of Assyria who were waiting to pour over the country. With dramatic force Amos thundered out his message.

> *Yahweh said to me, 'What do you see, Amos?' 'A plumb-line', I answered, and Yahweh said, 'I am setting a plumb-line to the heart of my people Israel; never again will I pass them by. The hill-shrines of Isaac shall be desolated and the sanctuaries of Israel laid waste; I will rise, sword in hand, against the house of Jeroboam'.* **(Amos 7:8-9)**

'What do you see, Amos?'

Amaziah, a priest of Bethel, reported to the king all that Amos had preached. 'The country cannot stand his words,' he pleaded. 'Get back to Judah,' they shouted at him. But Amos preached on, even telling Amaziah that his own wife would be carted off like a city strumpet!

Nobody had ever stated so clearly before the moral implications of Israel's religious covenant with Yahweh. If belief did not affect behaviour and shape business and political life it was useless and deserved to be swept away. Amos's sermons were never forgotten. The rough, uncompromising words of the shepherd were written down and mulled over, especially when the locusts of Assyria did start to move south twenty years later.

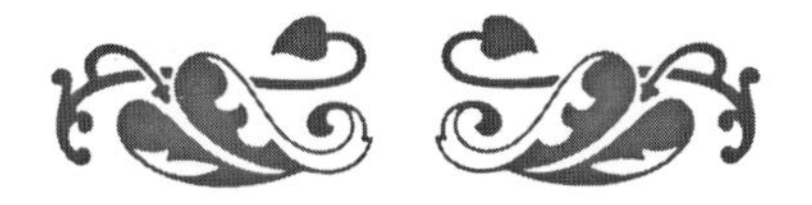

31 Hosea (745 BC)

Hosea 1–3; 4; 6–8; 10–11:5

LATE in the reign of Jeroboam II the message of Amos was taken up by another preacher, whose name was Hosea. Like Amos he preached in the northern kingdom of Israel, but unlike Amos he was a northerner himself, and consequently his preaching, though just as damning, was couched in more compassionate language.

Israel's preachers (*nabi*) often used symbols to convey the brunt of their message. For instance, Saul ripping Samuel's cloak was a symbol of the crown being torn away from Saul, and Amos saw in a plumb line Yahweh's moral gauge. Hosea's symbol came from a tragedy in his own life.

He married a woman called Gomer and had three children, all of whom he gave symbolic names to signify Yahweh's disappointment with his people. Then, abruptly, Gomer left him and went to live with a string of lovers. Hosea was devastated but never lost the love he had for his wife and sought to win her back home.

When she pursues her lovers she will not overtake them,
when she looks for them she will not find them;
then she will say,
'I will go back to my husband again;
I was better off with him than I am now.' **(Hosea 2:7)**

It was love that was steady and constant, and eventually he was successful in winning her back. From the depths of this experience Hosea saw a parallel of Yahweh's relationship with Israel. Though the nation had consistently overlooked the marriage it had with Yahweh, His love remained constant.

When Israel was a boy, I loved him;
I called my son out of Egypt:
but the more I called, the futher they went
from me . . . **(Hosea 11:1-2)**

Beginning with this parallel, Hosea outlines Israel's shortcomings.

The priests were unreliable:

Priest? By day and night you blunder on,
you and the prophet with you.
My people are ruined for lack of knowledge;
. . .
You have forgotten the teaching of God,
and I, your God, will forget your sons **(Hosea 4:5-6).**

Sacrifices were empty rituals:

loyalty is my desire, not sacrifice,
not whole-offerings but the knowledge of God **(Hosea 6:6).**

Too many people still flirted with Baal worship:

Your calf-gods stink, O Samaria;
my anger flares up against them.
. . .
For what sort of god is this bull?
It is no god,
a craftsman made it . . . **(Hosea 8:5-6)**

Kings were godless:

King after king falls from power,
but not one of them calls upon me **(Hosea 7:7).**

The courts were as comtemptible as in Amos's day:

There is nothing but talk,
imposing of oaths and making of treaties, all to no purpose;
and litigation spreads like a poisonous weed
along the furrows of the fields **(Hosea 10:4).**

Excessive booze scrambled the people's wits and orgies of temple prostitution were a national scandal.

Hosea's message was clear. Israel was facing imminent danger, which her spineless corruption made it impossible to resist. She had sown the wind and was about to reap the whirlwind. It was no good pleading to Egypt and Assyria, like a 'silly senseless pigeon' (Hosea 7:11). The day of reckoning had come.

O it's broke the lock and splintered the door,
O it's the gate where they're turning, turning;
Their boots are heavy on the floor
And their eyes are burning. **(W.H. Auden, *The Quarry*)**

The boots were those of the Assyrian hordes who, even as Hosea spoke, were relentlessly pummelling at the gates of Israel's northernmost cities.

32 The Fall of Israel (745–721 BC)

(Jeroboam II, Zechariah, Shallum, Menaham, Pekahiah, Pekah, Hoshea); 2 Kings 14:23–15:31; 17

THE last twenty-five years of the northern kingdom of Israel saw seven kings come and go. Jeroboam II reigned for forty-one years, but his son Zechariah enjoyed the purple for just six months, and only Menahem of the remaining five died in his bed. Menahem was a cruel man who ripped open all the pregnant women of Tappuah because the city resisted him, but he was unable to stem the tide of Assyrian aggression. When Tiglath-pileser invaded the country, Menahem was forced to pay an enormous tribute of a thousand talents of silver to pacify the Assyrian. He raised the sum by taxing all the wealthy men of Israel to the tune of fifty silver shekels each.

Pekah sought to throw off the Assyrian yoke by forming a defensive alliance with Rezin the king of Syria. Together they tried to compel King Ahaz of Judah to join them. The prophet Isaiah advised Ahaz against the alliance, calling Pekah and Rezin 'two smouldering stumps of firewood'. He was proved right, for both were soon murdered and the Assyrian steamroller moved remorselessly through Syria and Galilee, destroying Hazor and Gilead and taking all the land of Naphtali.

Hoshea, Israel's last king, made an abortive attempt to gain the aid of Egypt, but it was a last desperate throw doomed to failure. Shalmaneser V brought his Assyrian army to the walls of Samaria and began a siege which lasted for three years. He died during the siege, but his successor Sargon II finally breached the walls of Israel's capital city.

Some Israelites had avoided falling into Assyrian hands by escaping to Judah, taking religious and political scrolls with them which were deposited in Jerusalem. But, according to Sargon's record, 27,290 men were forced into exile. They resettled in distant parts of the Assyrian Empire where, away from the land they loved, they merged with other colonised people and completely lost their identity. Victims of Assyrian oppression from other lands were forcibly relocated to the Samaria region where eventually they fraternised and intermarried with remaining Israelites. This 'mixed' race was later contemptuously called 'Samaritans' by the 'pure' Hebrews of the south.

27,290 men were forced into exile.

The harrowing words of the shepherd preacher Amos had become historical fact.

> *Behold, I, the Lord God,*
> *have my eyes on this sinful kingdom,*
> *and I will wipe it off the face of the earth* **(Amos 9:8).**

The northern kingdom of Israel was no more.

33 Uzziah (Azariah) and Jotham (783–735 BC)

2 Kings 15:1-7; Isaiah 6

DURING the traumatic years of Assyria's rise to power, Judah had managed to avoid most of the agonies accompanying the fall of Syria and Israel. This was partly due to her geographical position but also to the great political stability she achieved through a firm faithfulness to the family of David. The frequent *coups d'état* in Israel, with the accompanying violence and intrigue, were avoided in Judah, who, apart from a brief hiccup during Queen Athaliah's day, always had a descendant of David on the throne. Things were not perfect in Judah, but at least men in authority slept soundly in their beds knowing that nobody was plotting an insurrection that could cost them their heads.

Judah's stability is well illustrated by the long reign of Uzziah (Azariah) who for half a century ruled the land. His achievements were many: he completely modernised the army and increased its efficiency; he regained control of commercial highways and the coastal regions of the Gaza strip; he built copper and iron works at Elath on the Red Sea, now called Eilat, a popular modern resort for sun worshippers; and he rebuilt parts of Jerusalem and took a personal interest in farming methods. The second book of Chronicles says Uzziah 'loved the soil'.

The only tragedy in Uzziah's life was a personal one—he was struck with leprosy and had to live the latter part of his reign separated from everybody in a private house. His son Jotham became regent in his father's stead, but the over-ruling influence over the land remained with Uzziah.

Uzziah's reign was an island of peace in times of uncertainty and turbulence. When he died, the future looked threatening. In the very year of his death, Isaiah of Jerusalem became a preacher.

34 Isaiah and King Ahaz (718 BC)

2 Kings 16; Isaiah 1; 5; 7–8

UZZIAH'S death after fifty years on the throne marked the end of an era. In the uncertainty of those days, when the whole world seemed to be 'in a terrible state o'chassis', Isaiah was praying in the temple when he had a religious experience so compelling that it changed his life. As he prayed he seemed to be lifted into the holy presence of Yahweh Himself and commissioned to speak on His behalf.

When the opportunity to preach came, the message was similar to that delivered to Israel by Amos. Looking at the empty religious rituals of Jerusalem, he cried out in Yahweh's name:

Your countless sacrifices, what are they to me?
. . .
I am sated with whole-offerings of rams
and the fat of buffaloes
. . .
The offer of your gifts is useless,
the reek of sacrifice is abhorrent to me.
. . .
Cease to do evil and learn to do right,
pursue justice and champion the oppressed;
give the orphan his rights, plead the widow's cause
(Isaiah 1:11-17).

The picture Isaiah paints of life in Judah is sad indeed. Rulers took bribes, the land was full of idols, the poor were oppressed, rich landowners grasped more, and some drank heavily from dawn to dusk. Passionately Isaiah cried,

Shame on you! you who drag wickedness along like
a tethered sheep
and sin like a heifer on a rope,

> . . .
> *Shame on you! you who call evil*
> *good and good evil . . .* **(Isaiah 5:18-20)**

Judah was a sinful nation, a race of evil-doers who had deserted the very principles for which they had been called to be a nation.

When Amos delivered his message to Israel, he did so rather like a visiting evangelist, but Isaiah's preaching was aimed at his own people. Furthermore, he spoke as one of the privileged classes who was accustomed to rubbing shoulders with ministers and civil servants, a man who had the ear of the king himself.

Young King Ahaz came to the throne in troubled days when Pekah of Israel and Rezin of Syria were doing their best to force Judah into an alliance against Assyria. Such was the king's distress that he sacrificed one of his sons in some vain attempt to placate whatever gods were angry with him. One day while he was checking on the city's water supply, Isaiah approached him with advice. It was, simply, that he was to stop fretting about possible alliances with other countries and put more trust in Yahweh. 'Your wife is with child,' he said, 'and by the time that child is born and is old enough to say "daddy" or "mummy" the dangers for Israel and Syria will be over.' The child would be a sign, he would be 'Immanuel', a symbol that 'God was with us'. But Ahaz was in no mood to listen to Isaiah. Faith was too nebulous. The unpleasant facts were that he had to join the alliance of Pekah and Rezin or get help from Assyria in order to get Israel and Syria off his back. He chose the latter course.

The Assyrian Tiglath-pileser did precisely what Ahaz required. He marched against Syria, killing Rezin and dividing his kingdom into provinces of the growing Assyrian Empire. Then he turned his attention on Pekah and annexed much of Israel's land, leaving the nation weak and dispirited. Ahaz rushed to Damascus to pay his toadying respects to the Assyrian, only to discover that he had 'saved' Judah at the cost of complete servitude to Tiglath-pileser. Such was Judah's humiliation that Assyrian altars were erected inside the temple at Jerusalem. Everything of worth was fleeced from the land and sent to Assyria whose hand rested heavily upon a once proud people.

In these miserable days Isaiah met Ahaz again as he stood by the gentle stream of Shiloah which carried vital water supplies from the Spring of Gihon to a pool inside the walls of Jerusalem. Gazing into the waters, Isaiah rebuked Ahaz for rejecting the gentle water of Shiloah in favour of the strong, flooding water of the Euphrates. The river of Assyria was about to sweep through Judah in a flood.

Dejected, Isaiah withdrew from public life for a time and joined prophetic colleagues in a retreat. Here some of his words were written down and remembered, and here he worked out his belief that Yahweh would still be faithful to the remnant in Judah who had kept faith in Him. This remnant (or 'church') would wait with hope for Yahweh to lift his heavy hand of judgement from the land.

35 *Micah (715 BC)*

2 Kings 16:1-4; Micah 1–6

THE defeat of Israel was a stunning blow to Yahwehists in north and south. After years of uncertainty the blow had fallen. Strange voices were heard in Israel's streets, signs of ruthless occupation appeared, and long-established families vanished from their villages overnight.

'The shadow of the morrow weighed on men' and on none more so than a farmer called Micah who lived in Judah at Moresheth, a small town close to the Philistine plain. Having witnessed the fall of Israel he took up the prophetic mantle, which Isaiah had temporarily laid down, and declared to Judah a message reminiscent to that of Amos. If the people were not ready to accept the moral demands of Yahweh then the fate of Judah would be no different to that of Israel. He spoke with massive authority on behalf of the yeoman farmers who were being exploited by commercial overlords:

> *Shame on those who lie in bed planning evil and wicked deeds*
> *and rise at daybreak to do them,*
> *knowing that they have the power!*
> *They covet land and take it by force;*
> *if they want a house they seize it;*
> *they rob a man of his home*
> *and steal everyman's inheritance* **(Micah 2:1-2)**.

Judah's rulers were as wicked as any that lived in Israel:

> *you flay men alive and tear the very flesh from their bones;*
> *you devour the flesh of my people,*
> *strip off their skin,*
> *splinter their bones;*
> *you shred them like flesh into a pot,*
> *like meat into a cauldron* **(Micah 3:2-3)**.

The religious leaders were not to be trusted either:

Her rulers sell justice,
her priests give direction in return for a bribe,
her prophets take money for their divination . . . **(Micah 3:11)**

Despite all the evidence of corruption, however, the people still cried:

'Is not Yahweh among us?' . . .
'then no disaster can befall us.' **(Micah 3:11)**

Micah declared that if things did not change the end was inevitable:

. . . on your account
Zion shall become a ploughed field,
Jerusalem a heap of ruins,
and the temple hill rough heath **(Micah 3:12).**

Micah carried the work of the eighth-century prophets to its logical conclusion. It was foolish to infer that because Yahweh had chosen Israel and Judah to be His people, they could behave as though there were no laws or justice. The bill would come in. Jerusalem and the temple did not guarantee Yahweh's favour, they only served to underline Judah's privileges, but privilege meant responsibility. Micah added his withering comments about religious sacrifices to those of Amos, Hosea and Isaiah.

What shall I bring when I approach Yahweh?
How shall I stoop before God on high?
Am I to approach him with whole-offerings
or yearling calves?
Will Yahweh accept thousands of rams
or ten thousand rivers of oil?
Shall I offer my eldest son for my own wrongdoing,
my children for my own sin?

God had told you what is good;
and what is it that Yahweh asks of you?
Only to act justly, to love loyalty,
to walk wisely before your God **(Micah 6:6-8).**

Scathing though Micah's words are, they are not without hope. Israel's greatest days had been under David, and Micah declared that from the great king's birthplace hope still shone:

But you Bethlehem in Ephrathah,
small as you are to be among Judah's clans,

out of you shall come forth a governor for Israel,
one whose roots are far back in the past . . . **(Micah 5:2)**

We are not always sure how contemporaries received the message of the prophets, but in Micah's case we know (thanks to the later prophet Jeremiah) that King Hezekiah listened to the spokesman for the poor and as a result instigated changes in Judah which did much to rectify the dreadful injustices spelled out by Micah of Moresheth. There was encouragement in that, but Assyria, 'the rod of Yahweh's anger' was still scouring the land hungry for conquest.

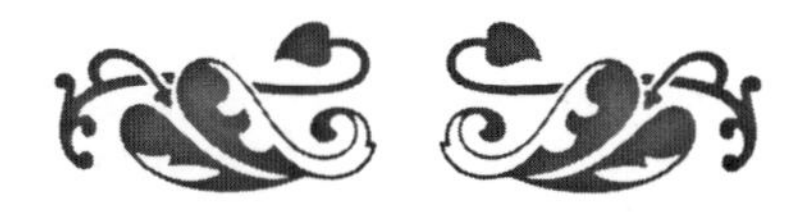

36 Isaiah and Hezekiah (715–687 BC)

2 Kings 18–19; Isaiah 9–10; 30–31; 36–37

AS Assyria devoured more and more smaller kingdoms so she became a formidable empire, but that did not prevent some nations from scheming her overthrow. Isaiah's words to those who looked towards Egypt for salvation were uncompromising:

> *Shame upon those who go down to Egypt for help*
> *and rely on horses,*
> *putting their trust in chariots many in number*
> *and in horsemen in their thousands,*
> *but do no look to the Holy One of Israel*
> *or seek guidance of Yahweh!* **(Isaiah 31:1)**

Isaiah disappeared from public life for a period during the latter part of the reign of Ahaz. Instead, he gathered disciples round him and passed on his teaching to this 'remnant' who would listen. His words were remembered and some of them written down. He prepared himself for a time when the nation would recognise the futility of seeking guidance from mediums and 'familiar spirits who squeak and gibber', and listen again to authentic preaching. Probably during this period Isaiah worked out his belief that Yahweh, the ancient God of Israel, was controlling the destinies of all the nations. Therefore, it was perfectly feasible that even Assyria was being used by Yahweh as 'a rod of anger' against Judah. The prophet's narrow conception of Yahweh broadened out from the purely national to the international, though the privileges and responsibilities of 'the chosen people' remained.

Then Ahaz died, and with the enthronement of his son Hezekiah, new optimism was born. The young king ruled sensibly and vigorously. When Assyria was occupied in struggles in other parts of the empire, Hezekiah instigated religious reforms which suppressed many of the local shrines still associated with Caananite practices and promoted Jerusalem as a unique centre for worship. He purified the temple which had been polluted by Assyrian accretions during his father's days.

These religious reforms sparked off a surge of patriotism and national enterprise which is well illustrated by the remarkable engineering achievement of the Siloam tunnel. Ahaz had long worried about Jerusalem's water supply, but Hezekiah did something about it. A tunnel 1,777 feet long was carved through solid rock to bring spring waters from outside Jerusalem to a pool inside the city wall. Workers started at both ends and met in the middle after following a winding route. The feat was commemorated on the famous Siloam inscription which recalls that:

> *While there was yet three cubits to be bored through, there was heard the voice of one calling unto another.*

Hezekiah symbolised the revival of national fervour, and even Isaiah described him as:

> *. . . a son given to us*
> *to bear the symbol of dominion on his shoulder;*
> *and he shall be called*
> *in purpose wonderful, in battle God-like,*
> *Father for all time, Prince of peace* **(Isaiah 9:6)**.

It was a reputation difficult to live up to, and it was not long before the gathering aspirations for a new Davidic era received a nasty shock. An anti-Assyrian rebellion, plotted in Egypt, gained support in Philistia and Hezekiah flirted with the idea of joining the revolt. Isaiah, desperately worried lest all Judah's recent gains should be lost, symbolically walked through Jerusalem's streets semi-naked and barefoot to signify the garb of prisoners of war. It was a timely warning, for in 711 BC Sargon's army marched south and destroyed the eye of the revolution at Ashdod. Judah shivered in anticipation of reprisals, but Isaiah's influence had saved Hezekiah from deep involvement in the revolt and Judah breathed again—but not for long.

Six years later Sargon II died and many parts of the empire tried to shake off the Assyrian oppression. This time Hezekiah could not resist joining in, despite Isaiah's warning. Sargon's successor, Sennacherib, marched south over-running the fortified cities of Judah. According to Sennacherib's annals, preserved on a magnificent hexagonal clay prism, forty-six cites were defeated, 200,150 people were taken captive and Hezekiah was shut within the walls of Jerusalem 'like a bird in a cage'. Strangely, at this point, Isaiah's advice to the king changes.

Previously he had thought all resistance to Assyria useless, but now that the army was actually at the gate, Isaiah advocated a passive but stubborn resistance:

> *Come back, keep peace, and you will be safe;*
> *in stillness and in staying quiet, there lies*
> *your strength* **(Isaiah 30:15)**.

Some tried to escape but Isaiah's call for calm resistance never wavered, even when the propaganda war began to heat up and Hezekiah weakened.

Sennacherib sent his ***Rabshakeh***, or chief officer, with the terms of surrender. Refusing to speak in Aramaic, the language of diplomacy, he shouted taunts in Hebrew making the hopelessness of Jerusalem's position clear. The ***Rabshekeh***'s voice boomed over the city walls:

> *'Do not listen to Hezekiah; . . . "Make peace with me. Come out to me, and then you shall each eat the fruit of his own vine and his own fig-tree, and drink the water of his own cistern . . . Beware lest Hezekiah mislead you by telling you that Yahweh will save you. Did the god of any of these nations save his land . . . ? Where are the gods of Samaria? Did they save Samaria . . . ?"'* **(Isaiah 36:16-19)**

Hezekiah was a troubled man but still Isaiah's advice remained the same:

> *'"Do not be alarmed . . . [by] the lackeys of the king of Assyria . . . "'* **(Isaiah 37:6)**

Then something remarkable happened. The Assyrian siege was abruptly called off and Sennacherib hurried back to Ninevah at the double. The unbelievable had happened. The citizens of Jerusalem, who had been looking down a gun barrel for so long, could not believe it. They said it was an answer to prayer; Yahweh's angels must have attacked the Assyrians during the night. There was a rumour of plague. Sennacherib's own records say nothing of the event, though it has been conjectured that an uprising in Babylonia compelled him to redeploy his troops.

Whatever the reason, Jerusalem had been miraculously saved at the eleventh hour. It was such a vivid experience to the citizens that it added another chapter to the saga of Hebrew history, a chapter which said that Zion was Yahweh's special city and He would never allow it to be violated. It was a belief which lasted for over a hundred years.

37 Mannaseh (687–642 BC)

2 Kings 21:1-18

JERUSLEM had been exposed to the full might of Assyria and survived to tell the tale. Yet Assyria still controlled the largest empire the world had ever seen, stretching from the Persian Gulf to Turkey in the north and the Mediterranean Sea in the west, and dominating the crescent of fertile land which bordered the Tigris and Euphrates rivers. Much has been written in biblical books about Assyrian terror inflicted upon defeated peoples, but it was psychological terror rather than mere sadism. Assyrian annals record that their kings often allowed soldiers to flee for their lives in order that they might get back home to spread the stories of invincible Assyrian warriors. It was a persuasive deterrent against possible rebellion.

Although Jerusalem had survived intact, Hezekiah's son Manasseh had little room for manoeuvre. Assyrian officials were on hand to watch for signs of disloyalty to the empire. Spies in discreet places kept the royal palace informed, and one Assyrian king said:

> *The man who loves the house of his lords, opens the ears of his lords to whatever he sees or hears. it is good that you have sent a message and opened my ears.*

These 'eyes' and 'ears', the equivalent of today's phone taps, were an irritation to subject peoples such as Judah, as were the irksome taxes, but if vassal states toed the line then life was tolerable. Manasseh toed the line. Unlike his father Hezekiah, he tolerated worship at the old shrines 'on every high hill and under every green tree' and Canaanite practices, which included sacred prostitution and human sacrifice. In addition the cults of the Assyrians attracted many in Judah, and astrology, magic and spiritualism all received official sanction.

He [Manasseh] built altars for all the host of heaven in the two courts of the house of Yahweh; he made his son pass through the fire, he practised soothsaying and divination, and dealt with ghosts and spirits **(2 Kings 21:5-6)**.

Manasseh seemed prepared to do anything to accommodate his Assyrian overlords.

Belief in the power of demons seeped into Judah's thinking at this time, for they were a prominent feature of Assyrian religion. Demons were to be found everywhere, but especially in deserts, graveyards and ruined buildings, and they were particularly active when women were giving birth.

Manasseh seemed prepared to do anything to accommodate his Assyrian overlords. It was a policy that kept him on the throne for fifty-five years, but the abiding memory people had of him was of weakness and wickedness.

. . . Manasseh misled them into wickedness far worse than that of the nations which Yahweh had exterminated in favour of the Israelites . . . [he] shed so much innocent blood that he filled Jerusalem full to the brim . . . **(2 Kings 21:9-16)**

Yet still the faithful followed Yahweh, diligently obeying the laws of Moses and writing down prophetic words that would inspire future generations. Among these were the zealous Rechabites, who, a century later, were warmly commended by Jeremiah for their faith during Judah's dark age.

38 Zephaniah (640–638 BC)

Zephaniah 1–3

EARLY in the reign of Manasseh's grandson, Josiah, another prophet, startled the people of Jerusalem with a tirade as doom-laden as that of any prophet before him. His name was Zephaniah, and the book named after him is brief and uncompromising.

Amos had warned Israelites that crying piously for the 'Day of Yahweh' was like bringing judgement crashing onto your own head, and now Zephaniah brought a similar message for Jerusalem. A mediaeval artist painted the prophet as a man with a lantern scouring the streets of the city for sinners doomed to destruction:

I will search Jerusalem with a lantern
and punish all who sit in stupor over the dregs of wine,
. . .

'I will search Jerusalem with a lantern.'

The great day of Yahweh is near,
it comes with speed;
no runner so fast as that day,
no raiding band so swift.
That day is a day of wrath,
a day of anguish and affliction,
a day of destruction and devastation,
a day of murk and gloom,
a day of cloud and dense fog,
a day of triumph and battle-cry
over fortified cities and lofty
battlements **(Zephaniah 1:12-16)**.

Nobody was safe. Yahweh's patience with his stiff-necked people was at an end. Therefore, from the Fish Gate at the top of the city, through the narrow alleys where merchants peddled their wares, down to the Lower Town, all these crooks would be wiped out.

Despite the vehement language, however, there is hope for a remnant, just as Isaiah had declared:

On that day, Jerusalem,
. . .
. . . I will rid you
of your proud and arrogant citizens,
and never again shall you flaunt your pride
on my holy hill **(Zephaniah 3:11)**.

In Zephaniah's day the Assyrian star was waning quickly, so it is uncertain whom he saw as Yahweh's agent 'to sweep the earth clean'. What is certain, however, is that the love of God could not light up the city until all that was filthy and foul had been scoured out. His message echoed down the draughty passages of Jerusalem:

Seek Yahweh,
all in the land who live humbly by his laws,
seek righteousness, seek a humble heart;
it may be that you will find shelter
in the day of Yahweh's anger **(Zephaniah 2:3)**.

39 Josiah and the Deuteronomic Revolution (640–609 BC)

2 Kings 22–23:30; 2 Chronicles 34–35; Deuteronomy 12–26

MANASSEH'S grandson, Josiah, came to the throne as an eight-year-old boy-king and reigned for thirty-one years. They were years which saw a rapid decline in Assyrian authority. The Assyrians remained the major force in Middle Eastern affairs, but they found it ever more difficult to maintain their borders, especially against Babylonians and the Medes who squeezed them ceaselessly from the east. This preoccupation with their eastern border gave Judah respite, and as Josiah grew older so he increased in confidence and began to stiffen his resistance to Assyria. He moved his sphere of influence northward into land that had once been the northern kingdom of Israel and hopes of a new dynamic kingdom, ruled by a second David, stirred the imagination and re-awakened nationalistic fervour. As with Hezekiah, the new nationalism coincided with religious reforms, and Josiah enthusiastically set about ridding the temple of pagan accretions.

During this 'spring clean' a discovery was made which became the focal point of Josiah's reforms and later a major factor in shaping the presentation of Old Testament history. The high-priest Hilkiah found a scroll of law (*torah*) hidden away in the temple and it was passed on to the king. As he read it, Josiah became convinced that this discovery was nothing less than the command of Yahweh to his people. It affirmed that all the Canaanite and Assyrian customs that had seeped into Israel's religion were contrary to Yahweh's commands and should be ripped

Hilkiah found a scroll of law hidden away in the temple.

out of the nation's life. In practical terms, what this meant was that all sacred shrines outside Jerusalem were to be destroyed.

> *. . . [Josiah] desecrated the hill-shrines where they had burnt sacrifices, from Geba to Beersheba, and dismantled the hill-shrines of the demons . . . He destroyed the horses that the kings of Judah had set up in honour of the sun at the entrance to the house of Yahweh . . .* **(2 Kings 23:8-11)**

> *At Bethel he dismantled the altar by the hill-shrine made by Jeroboam . . . he broke its stones in pieces, crushed them to dust and burnt the sacred pole* **(2 Kings 23:15)**.

All sacrifices were to be vigorously supervised in the capital city by an 'official' priesthood. Their job was to ensure that Judah's religion was cleansed of those defiling alloys which for generations had weakened the nation's will. Essentially, the reforms were conservative, looking back to Moses as the architect of Israel's life, and to slavery in Egypt as the birthplace of the nation. In an attempt to reforge links with these origins, the long-neglected Passover was re-instituted. It seemed to people in Josiah's day that Israel was being reborn and a solemn Covenant service was convened amid great emotion.

The service was reminiscent of the ancient Covenant renewal of Joshua at Shechem, and it has been suggested that the 'new' Torah had its origins in Shechem and was moved south when the northern kingdom of Israel fell to Assyria in 721 BC. If this was so, the idea of sacrifice being centralised would have originally applied to Shechem and not Jerusalem.

It is now widely accepted that the 'new' Torah found in the temple, was a substantial part of the book now called Deuteronomy ('second law'). Jerusalem is not mentioned, but the notion of a central sanctuary is undoubtedly a major theme of that book. Once the concepts of this 'new' Torah had been digested, therefore, a fundamental re-think had to take place, not merely about conventional practice, but also about the nation's past. Consequently, just as Russia's history was re-written according to Marxist/Leninist ideas after the 1917 Revolution, so was Israel's after Josiah's Deuteronomic Revolution. The nation's long saga was re-worked, and wherever past kings were thought to have sympathised with Canaanite customs, especially Jeroboam I, they were roundly condemned as those who

> *followed in the footsteps of Jeroboam and led my people Israel into sin . . .* **(2 Kings 10:29; 13:2-11; 14:24; *et passim*)**

Josiah's reign, in the short term, revitalised the nation and his revolution gave a stimulus to Yahwehism. But in retrospect the Deuteronomic interpretation of history was too narrow. The concentration on Torah and Temple put Yahweh into a straitjacket and made belief in Him naïve and predictable. After all, a god whose ways are *fully* understood is a god too small to worship.

The euphoria of the revolution was short-lived. The sun of Assyria waned ever faster before the onslaught of Babylon, and the great capital city of Assyria fell in 612 BC. Then the unexpected and the unthinkable happened. The Egyptian Pharaoh Necho, alarmed at the growing strength of Babylon, marched north to assist Assyria. Josiah moved to intercept him and in the resulting clash in the pass of Megiddo, Judah's forces were defeated. Judah's king, not yet forty years old, was executed and the dreams of a generation perished with him.

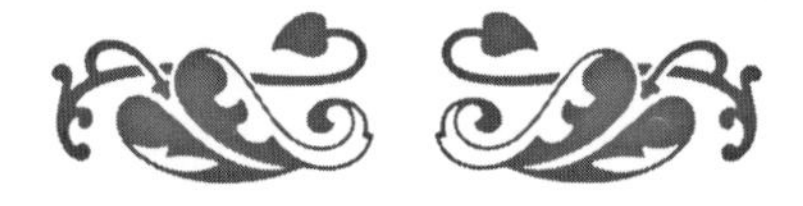

40 Nahum (612 BC)

Nahum 1–3

IN 612 BC, three years before the death of Josiah at Megiddo, the ancient world was aghast at news that Assyria's capital city Ninevah had fallen. While under siege from the combined forces of Babylonians and Medes (a new nation from the mountains of Iran), a flood from the River Tigris swept away part of the city wall making it indefensible. Ninevah was over-run and so thoroughly laid waste that for over 2,000 years the wonder of that city lay buried beneath the soil of Iraq. Not until the nineteenth century were the colossal winged bulls and lions unearthed and housed in the British Museum and the Louvre to give us an inkling of the majesty that was once Ninevah.

After the initial shock came the rejoicing, and a man called Nahum captured the feeling of the time:

> *. . . O King of Assyria,*
> *. . .*
> *Your wounds cannot be assuaged, your injury is mortal;*
> *all who have heard of your fate clap their hands in joy*
> **(Nahum 3:18-19).**

There is nothing profound or spiritual in Nahum's words, which pour out in pitiless glee at the thought of Assyria's chickens coming home to roost:

> *squadrons of horses advance on the city in mad frenzy;*
> *they jostle one another in the outskirts, like waving torches;*
> *the leaders display their prowess*
> *as they dash to and fro like lightning,*
> *rushing in headlong career;*
> *they hasten to the wall, and mantelets are set in position.*
> *The sluices of the rivers are opened, the palace topples down;*

the train of captives goes into exile,
their slave-girls are carried off,
moaning like doves and beating their breasts;
and Ninevah has become like a pool of water.

. . .

'Stop! Stop!' they cry; but none turns back **(Nahum 2:4-8)**.

The plight of Ninevah in particular sends Nahum into raptures of venomous spleen:

Ah! blood-stained city, steeped in deceit,
full of pillage, never empty of prey!
Hark to the crack of the whip,
the rattle of the wheels and stamping of horses,
bounding chariots, chargers rearing,
swords gleaming, flash of spears!
The dead are past counting, their bodies lie in heaps,

. . .

'Ninevah is laid waste; who will console her?' **(Nahum 3:1-7)**

In those days of unrestrained glee, how could Nahum have foreseen that in one short generation the sweet would turn to sour, joy to weeping, and Jerusalem the golden would sink into the same dust as Ninevah?

The dead are past counting, their bodies lie in heaps.

41 *Habakkuk (605 BC)*

Habakkuk 1–3; Jeremiah 46

THE fall of Assyria threw the Middle East into confusion. Josiah's death at Pharaoh Necho's hand prompted the Egyptians to make a final attempt to establish an empire in the fertile crescent. He marched northward. Babylon, still swollen from devouring Assyria, moved westward to meet him. The confrontation took place in 605 BC at Carchemish in what is now southern Turkey and Babylon, under the command of Nebuchadnezzar, won a decisive victory. Egypt, in full retreat, sped homeward through Judah, leaving the prophet Jeremiah to say:

> *. . . they too turned and fled,*
> *not one of them stood his ground,*
> *The hour of his downfall has come upon them*
> *their day of reckoning* **(Jeremiah 46:21)**.

Clearly, Babylon was the new master of the world, and not one whit less ruthless or dominating than Assyria had been.

The outlook was bleak. Natural justice was everywhere being flouted, and violence ruled with an iron fist. Bewildered, a prophet called Habakkuk cried out in anguish:

> *How long, O Yahweh, have I cried to thee, unanswered?*
> *I cry, 'Violence!', but thou dost not save.*
> *Why dost thou let me see such misery,*
> *why countenance wrongdoing?*
> *. . .*
> *justice does not come forth victorious;*
> *for the wicked outwit the righteous,*
> *and so justice comes out perverted* **(Habakkuk 1:2-4)**.

Habakkuk's fear in the face of advancing ruthless armies can be well understood:

Their whole army advances, violence in their hearts;
a sea of faces rolls on;
they bring in captives countless as the sand.
...
they despise every fortress,
they raise siege-works and capture it **(Habakkuk 1:9-10)**.

Before such devastating and irresistible power Habakkuk beats on the gates of heaven with his prayers, demanding to know why Yahweh allows evil men to toy with the righteous like fish in a net. It is a prayer repeated years later by Job and in our own time by Jews in Auschwitz.

Lord! When wilt Thou save the people?

(Ebenezer Elliott, 1850)

Habakkuk finds no ready answers, but quells his despair by standing square on the 'watchtower of faith'.

The reckless will be unsure of himself,
while the righteous man will live by being faithful
(Habakkuk 2:4).

It was a faith about to be tested to the utmost by the fiery ordeal due to begin.

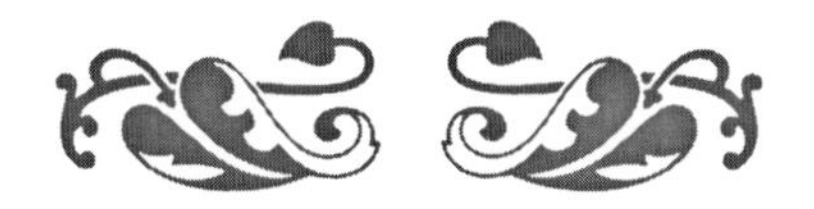

The Babylonians

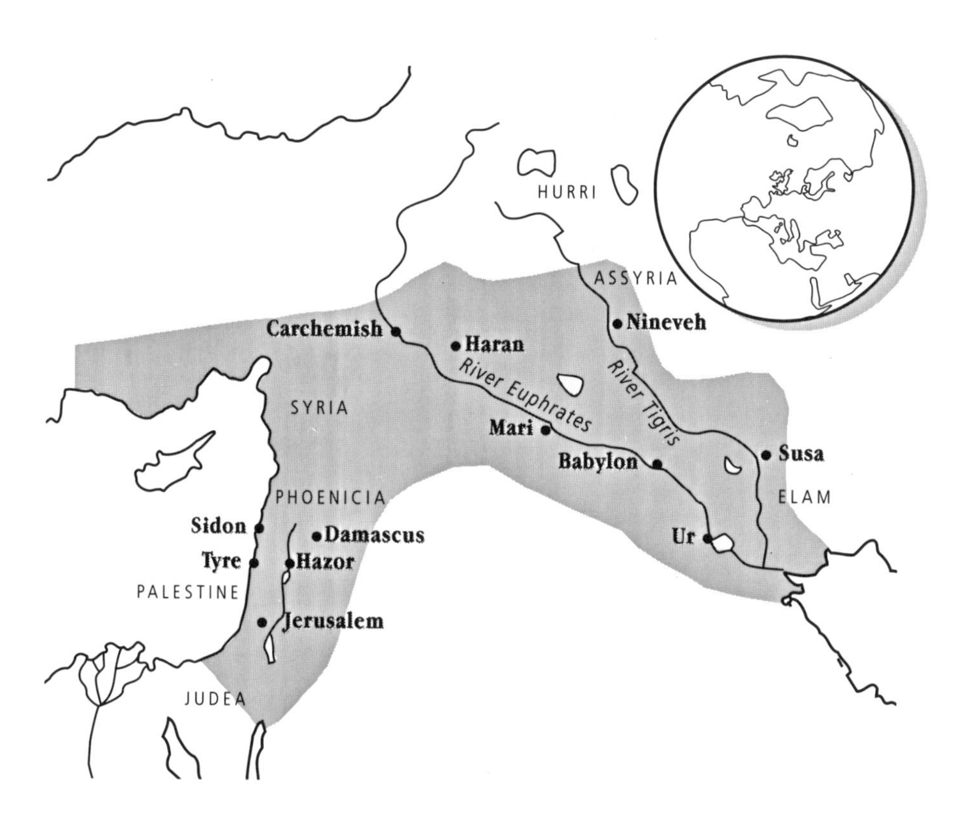

THE first Babylonian Empire stretches back to a period some 500 years before Abraham and reached a peak of excellence under the great king Hammurabi. Under this enlightened man the Babylonians conceived a code of law that applied to the whole of society, and thus removed the need or the excuse for personal vengeance and family vendettas. By the standards of present-day justice, Hammurabi's laws were rough and ready, but they established the principle of human rights that applied to all, even slaves. His empire included the regions of Syria in the west, Assyria in the north and Elam in the east, and was organised into provinces, ruled by governors but responsible to the king.

The empire declined after Hammurabi and was not truly revived for another thousand years when the second Babylonian Empire rose to meet the challenge of Assyria. This was the period that saw Babylon rebuilt with magnificent eighteen-kilometre walls, enormous ziggurats (which the Jews called the Tower of Babel) and the legendary hanging gardens, one of the wonders of the ancient world. The gateways to this enormous city, which enclosed 200,000 people, were lined with glazed blue bricks and decorated with huge reliefs of bulls and dragons.

Bricklayers, carpenters, spinners, metalsmiths and all such craftsmen were highly regarded in the empire and were only inferior to nobles. The detailed laws about trade and contracts indicates a society thriving with private enterprise and the accompanying commerce, which created a moneylender's paradise.

Marduk was the great god of the Babylonians, who had killed a rival, Tiamat, by using the storm and wind. But Babylon was fertile ground for the purveyors of omens, dreams and astrological signs. One record says, 'If in the month of Ab the thunder god casts his mouth, there will be gloom in the land.' It was from such astrological predictions that horoscopes developed.

The people of Babylon lived well and there can be little doubt that once the Jews had overcome the shock of being ripped away from their homeland, the exiles enjoyed a far higher standard of living than that in Judah. Jeremiah the prophet was not 'crying for the moon' when he encouraged the exiles to:

> *Build houses and live in them;*
> *plant gardens and eat their produce* **(Jeremiah 29:5)**.

42 Nebuchadnezzar Conquers Judah (605–562 BC)

(Jehoahaz, Jehoiakim, Jehoiachin and Zedekiah); 2 Kings 23:31–25

HOPES of a new 'golden age' died with Josiah at Megiddo. The great king's death introduced political confusion similar to that endured by the northern kingdom before she fell to Assyria. Jehoahaz, Josiah's son, was anointed king, but Pharaoh Necho allowed him only three months before carting him off to Egypt and replacing him with another son, Jehoiakim. He licked foreign boots to keep power and then, once established, became a tyrant to his own people. Under him Judah returned to heavy taxes, forced labour, fear, uncertainty and murder. He killed Uriah, a Yahwehist prophet, and would have done the same to the great Jeremiah had not the prophet's friends saved him.

When the Egyptian army was decisively defeated by the Babylonians at Carchemish in 605 BC, Jehoiakim bowed to the new master of the world—Nebuchadnezzar. He was tolerated for some years until the Babylonian began to sniff a Jewish rebellion. Then, quick as lightning, he marched south ravaging Judah and destroying isolated Egyptian outposts. Jehoiakim was killed and this left his eighteen-year-old son, Jehoiachin, to organise whatever resistance he could to the Babylonian ***blitzkrieg***. It was a forlorn hope.

> *At that time the troops of Nebuchadnezzar king of Babylon advanced on Jerusalem and besieged the city . . . He carried the people of Jerusalem into exile, the officers and the fighting men, ten thousand in number, together with all the craftsmen and smiths; only the weakest class of people were left. He deported Jehoiachin to Babylon . . .* **(2 Kings 24:10-15)**

The poor remnant left in Jerusalem were governed by Jehoiachin's uncle, Zedekiah, the last of David's line to rule over Judah. He managed to steer a quiet course for some nine years until, pursuing some death wish, he made a bid to overthrow Nebuchadnezzar's oppression. The response was immediate and terrible. Advancing with a formidable army, Nebuchadnezzar erected towers against the walls of Jerusalem. For two dreadful years the siege continued until the people were starved into submission.

> *The sucking infant's tongue*
> *cleaves to its palate from thirst;*
> *young children beg for bread*
> *but no one offers them a crumb.*
> *Those who once fed delicately*
> *are desolate in the streets,*
> *and those nurtured in purple*
> *now grovel on dunghills.*
>
> . . .
>
> *Tender-hearted women with their own hands*
> *boiled their own children;*
> *their children became their food*
> *in the day of my people's wounding* **(Lamentations 4:4-10)**.

The gates were thrown open and the Babylonians rushed in. Zedekiah escaped in the confusion:

> *But the Chaldaean army pursued the king and overtook him in the lowlands of Jericho . . . The king was seized and brought before the king of Babylon at Riblah . . . Zedekiah's sons were slain before his eyes; then his eyes were put out, and he was brought to Babylon in fetters of bronze* **(2 Kings 25:5-7)**.

The magnificent temple of Solomon was burnt to the ground.

The magnificent temple of Solomon, one of the wonders of the ancient world, was burnt to the ground and all the precious furniture was transported to Babylon. City walls and houses were bulldozed and Jerusalem the golden had become a heap of rubble. It seemed certain that the saga of Israel's history had come to an abrupt and sorry end. In the midst of the chaos and carnage, Jeremiah, one of Israel's greatest prophets, wept for his people.

> *I saw the earth, and it was without form and void;*
> *the heavens, and their light was gone.*
> *I saw the mountains, and they reeled;*
> *all the hills rocked to and fro.*
> *I saw, and there was no man,*
> *and the very birds had taken flight.*
> *I saw, and the farm-land was wilderness,*
> *and the towns all razed to the ground,*
> *before Yahweh in his anger* **(Jeremiah 4:22-26)**.

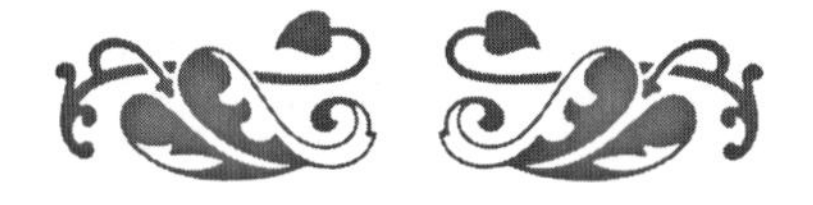

43 Jeremiah and Jehoiakim (609–598 BC)

2 Kings 23:36–24; Jeremiah 1–22:26; 36

FOR forty fateful years, from the heady days of King Josiah's reformation to the desperate days of defeat and exile, the prophet Jeremiah preached in Jerusalem. He was a lonely and sensitive man whose independence of thought enabled him to read, more accurately than most, the political and social situation of his day. He had faithful friends, but for the most part his words fell on deaf ears. Had Jeremiah been heeded, the subsequent history of Israel could well have been less tragic.

As a young man he shared in the euphoria of Josiah's religious revival, then, when Josiah was killed and enthusiasm waned, his preaching pointed out the shortcomings in Judah's national life:

> *Go up and down the streets of Jerusalem*
> *and see for yourselves;*
> *search her wide squares:*
> *can you find any man who acts justly,*
> *who seeks the truth . . . ?* **(Jeremiah 5:1)**

Religious practices, banned by Josiah, crept back into favour and Jeremiah scathingly attacked priests and prophets who said:

> *. . . 'You are our father' to a block of wood*
> *and cry, 'Mother' to a stone* **(Jeremiah 2:27)**.

These gods were no more able to speak 'than a scarecrow in a plot of cucumbers'. Like Martin Luther King, prophets cried, 'I have a dream, a dream, a dream,' but Jeremiah heard their words as their own inventions.

> *prophets and priests are frauds,*
> *every one of them;*
> *they dress my people's wound, but skin-deep only,*

with their saying, 'All is well.'
All well? Nothing is well! **(Jeremiah 8:10-11)**

How could it be well when King Jehoiakim had re-introduced child sacrifice into the Valley of Ben-hinnom and forced labour into the nation's life? Jeremiah's word for the king was totally uncompromising.

Shame on the man who builds his house by unjust means
and completes its roof-chambers by fraud,
making his countrymen work without payment,
giving them no wage for their labour!
Shame on the man who says, 'I will build a spacious house
with airy roof-chambers,
set windows in it, panel it with cedar
and paint it with vermilion'!
If your cedar is more splendid,
does that prove you a king?
Think of your father: he ate and drank,
dealt justly and fairly; all went well with him.
He dispensed justice to the lowly and poor;
did this not show he knew me? says Yahweh
(Jeremiah 22:13-16).

Such was Jeremiah's contempt for the king, he declared that when Jehoiakim died his burial would be treated with as much respect as that of a dead ass.

Not content with preaching the need for a moral revival, the prophet also had words about Judah's political posturings. Climbing to the temple courtyard he harangued passers-by with a simple message—if Judah did not learn some sense and make their lives square up to the laws of Yahweh, one day the much-esteemed temple would be destroyed just as thoroughly as Shiloh had been destroyed in Samuel's day. Not surprisingly, the priests were so angry that they immediately condemned him to death. Had it not been for a prince called Ahikim, Jeremiah's life would have ceased there and then. As it was, he was advised by his friends to keep a low profile for a period.

Undaunted, Jeremiah dictated the sermons to his secretary Baruch, who copied out his words onto a scroll. Baruch then went to the temple precincts and read out the prophet's words. They caused much consternation among the officers and people and the scroll was immediately taken to the king. Jehoiakim was relaxing in his winter palace with a fire burning in a brazier in front of him. As Jeremiah's words were read out, column by column, the king, despite protests from his advisers, arrogantly cut off lengths of the scroll and threw them into the fire until the whole of it was destroyed. He wanted to silence the prophet once and for all, but again his friends hid him away.

Jeremiah could not hide for long. His words were like a fire burning inside him and soon he was preaching again, though now his threats were more specific. He saw clearly that Judah's foreign policy, which refused to recognise the enormous strength of Babylon, was disastrous.

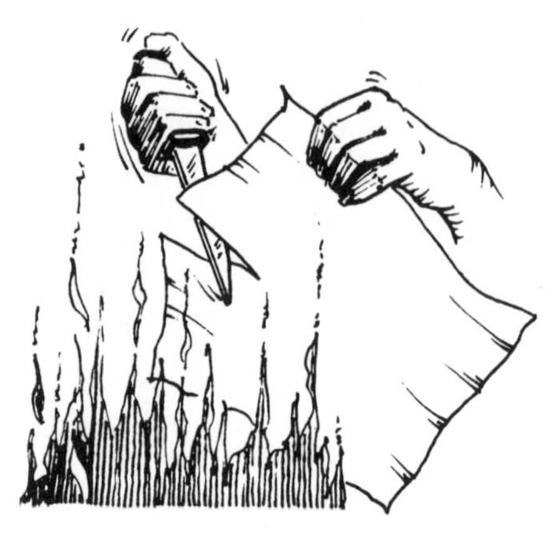

The king cut off lengths of the scroll and threw them into the fire.

> *The word of Yahweh came to me a second time: 'What is it that you see?' 'A cauldron', I said, 'on a fire, fanned by the wind; it is tilted away from the north.' Yahweh said:*
>
> *From the north disaster shall flare up*
> *against all who live in this land . . .* **(Jeremiah 1:13-14)**

Signs began to accompany Jeremiah's preaching. He went down to the Valley of Hinnom where human sacrifice was taking place, and having gathered an audience he chose his moment to smash a clay flask into pieces, demonstrating eloquently how Jerusalem would be smashed into pieces. Pashhur, the chief officer of the temple, was so incensed by this acted sermon the he had Jeremiah whipped and put into stocks for the night.

The prophet's dilemma was acute. The more he preached, the less people listened. If he refrained, the more his anguish boiled up inside him and the certainty of disaster drew closer. Jehoiakim hastened that disaster. He withheld tribute from Nebuchadnezzar in a reckless bid for independence. The Babylonians responded by sweeping through Judah like a sandstorm. In the ensuing chaos Jehoiakim was killed, Jerusalem capitulated and all the aristocrats, civil servants and princes were forced into exile in Babylon.

Jeremiah's warnings had been thoroughly vindicated. Surely people would listen to him now?

44 Jeremiah and Zedekiah (597–586 BC)

Jeremiah 24; 27–35; 37–44; 52

JEREMIAH'S lessons should have been heeded, but Baruch's memoirs of the prophet show clearly that while his prestige increased, Judah's political outlook remained unchanged. Zedekiah might have been a sound king in quieter times but though he often sought the advice of Jeremiah in secret, he was not strong enough to resist the self-destructive urge for nationalism whipped up by Judah's new politicians.

Jeremiah's message was consistent. It was as useless to resist Babylon's overwhelming power as to hold back Jordan. So one day when rebellion was being hatched between Zedekiah and envoys from Edom, Moab, Ammon, Tyre and Sidon, Jeremiah met them wearing a wooden yoke round his neck to signify the yoke of bondage they had to endure. Another prophet, called Hananiah, was advocating resistance to Babylon, so he smashed the yoke to signify that oppression would soon be over. Jeremiah had the last word by visiting the blacksmith's and having an iron yoke made!

Still restless he wrote a letter to the exiles in Babylon advising them to settle down and make the most of their situation:

> *Build houses and live in them; plant gardens and eat their produce. Marry wives and beget sons and daughters . . . and you may increase there and not dwindle away. Seek the welfare of any city to which I have carried you off, and pray to Yahweh for it; on its welfare your welfare will depend* **(Jeremiah 29:5-7)**.

He saw hope for the future with the exiles in Babylon rather than with those people still in Jerusalem. He made that clear in a telling sermon illustrated by two baskets of figs, one good, one bad:

> *I count the exiles of Judah...as good as these good figs . . . But Zedekiah . . . and the survivors of Jerusalem . . . —all these I will treat as bad figs . . . so bad that they are not fit to eat* **(Jeremiah 24:5-8)**.

His disgust at the political duplicity in Jerusalem increased when a law was passed freeing all the Hebrews from slavery (probably so that they could join the militia in the struggle against Babylon), only for it to be rescinded when Babylon's siege was lifted temporarily. Such two-faced hypocrisy deserved the worst possible fate. Jeremiah was not without hope for the future and was prepared to buy land as a stake in that future, but with the Babylonians at the gates of the city he was flogged and imprisoned. Some wanted him executed.

> *Then the officers said to the king, 'The man must be put to death. By talking in this way he is discouraging the soldiers and the rest of the people left in the city. He is pursuing not the people's welfare but their ruin.' . . . So they took Jeremiah and threw him into the pit in the court of the guard-house, letting him down with ropes. There was no water in the pit, only mud, and Jeremiah sank in the mud* **(Jeremiah 38:4-7).**

Jerusalem at this time was under siege and conditions inside the walls were horrifying. Those who died quickly were the lucky ones. Many died slowly from starvation:

> *. . . their faces turned blacker than soot,*
> *and no one knew them in the streets . . .* **(Lamentations 4:8)**

After two years, continued resistance was impossible and proud Jerusalem threw open her gates. Zion, the city of God and the city of David was reduced to rubble. Jeremiah's worst fears had become reality.

Yet even in the face of such appalling grief and devastation, the blind nationalism that had wreaked such havoc refused to be quenched. Gedaliah, a benevolent Jew who had been set up as a governor for the Babylonians, was assassinated. Against his will Jeremiah was dragged off to Egypt with other refugees and forced to live his last years in exile.

Against his will Jeremiah was dragged off to Egypt.

Jeremiah's bitter experience convinced him that Israel was incapable, and had always been incapable, of fulfilling her side of the covenant with Yahweh and therefore Yahweh had destroyed his people. He had destroyed but he could remake. Things could improve despite the holocaust and some day Israel would learn. A generation would emerge, more sensitive to the call of Yahweh, who would initiate a new beginning. A new covenant would be drawn up, not written on tablets of stone but in men's hearts.

> *I will set my law within them and write it on their hearts; I will become their God and they shall become my people. No longer need they teach one another to know Yahweh; all of them, high and low alike, shall know me, says Yahweh, for I will forgive their wrongdoing and remember their sin no more* **(Jeremiah 31:33-34)**.

Jeremiah had lived through some of the most dreadful years of Jewish history. He had known anger, frustration, fear and despair, but his last word, when it came, was one of hope.

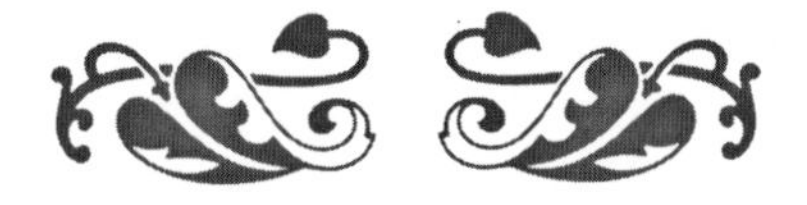

45 Ezekiel (597–575 BC)

Ezekiel 1–5; 8–9; 11–12; 18; 24; 37

THE southern kingdom of Judah had reached its lowest ebb and the crucial question was: What would happen to the country now that the cream of the nation had been transported to Babylon? Exiles from the northern kingdom had melted into Assyrian life, leaving only a mongrel community around Samaria, disparagingly called 'Samaritans' by those in the south who thought themselves 'pure'. Today only 400 Samaritans remain, some of whom, ironically, show sad signs of illness due to the closed marriage system among them. They still claim that their law of Moses is the oldest hand-written copy of the Torah in existence.

Unlike the Assyrian exiles, those in Babylon earnestly preserved their identity, collecting their sacred scrolls of law and maintaining their history, poems and traditions. Only at this point of history is it accurate to call these people 'Jews' because the word literally means 'descendants of the Judeans'. In exile many cherished this ancestry and still do.

Included in the first wave of exiles to Babylon in 597 BC were the aristocrats, and among these was the prophet Ezekiel. He came from priestly stock and settled around Nippur, a few miles from the great city of Babylon itself, with its spectacular double walls, hanging gardens and superb tower, or ziggurat, rebuilt by Nebuchadnezzar. In the midst of such magnificence Jerusalem must have seemed a million miles away.

By the rivers of Babylon we sat down and wept
when we remembered Zion.
There on the willow-trees
we hung up our harps,
for there those who carried us off
demanded music and singing,

and our captors called on us to be merry:
'Sing us one of the songs of Zion.'
How could we sing Yahweh's song
in a foreign land? **(Psalm 137:1-4)**

Ezekiel's trance-like prophecies reflect something of his new surroundings, but much more of his memories of Jerusalem. His knowledge of Zion is intimate and his prophecies suggest that he kept in touch with developments, even from 500 miles away. He seems as well informed about intrigues as Jeremiah, and just as aware of the smouldering fires of nationalism which burned deeply. Central to these nationalist dreams was the young king Jehoiachin who was under house arrest in Babylon. Ezekiel, with first-hand experience of Babylon's power, was as adamant as Jeremiah that thoughts of overthrowing that power were pipe dreams that contained within them the seeds of disaster.

Ezekiel's commission to prophesy came in a vision like that of Isaiah. There was the same awareness of the holiness of Yahweh, the same attendant cherubim with their mixture of human and animal attributes, and the same fear and unworthiness in the prophet. In addition, Ezekiel sees a strange vehicle with wheels shaped to move in any direction, sensitive to the winds of the spirit. It is this spirit that throws the prophet into ecstatic trances that in turn prompt his messages. His first prophecies concern the fall of Jerusalem: he draws pictures on tiles to illustrate a siege; ties himself up and eats meagre rations to simulate the conditions of his beleaguered kinsmen; and breaks a hole in the side of his house and carries out his belongings as though leaving for exile. On another occasion he cut off his hair and beard and weighed it before dividing it into three piles, leaving only a few wisps wrapped up in his cloak. One pile he threw onto a fire, another he slashed to pieces with a sword, and the other he cast into the wind, signifying the kind of disaster about to descend, leaving only a remnant safe. Even the death of Ezekiel's wife, the 'dearest thing' in his life, he uses as a sign to his people.

Then, as though in a holy chariot, Ezekiel is transported to different parts of Jerusalem to see, through Yahweh's eyes, the sins of the city uncovered. There were a few untainted and these receive a mark on their forehead to distinguish them, but overall the indictment is so damning that the vision closes with the glory of Yahweh leaving the city.

Not surprisingly, this strange man was never short of an audience. He was regarded as 'a good turn', a 'singer of fine songs', but the content of his preaching was ignored. Despite Jeremiah in Jerusalem and Ezekiel in exile, lessons would not be learned until they had been taught 'in fire and blood and anguish'.

Jerusalem was burned to the ground in 586 BC and soon new emigrés poured into Babylon with horrific tales of Zion's last hours. Ezekiel's dreams had become reality. The worst that could have happened had happened. From this moment, the prophet's message changed. In the blackest of nights Ezekiel began to point out the stars and speak with renewed hope. Jeremiah had painted a graphic picture of the Valley of Ben-hinnom where human corpses were food for the birds, but now Ezekiel prophesied that these dry bones would live again.

> *. . . as I prophesied there was a rustling sound and the bones fitted themselves together. As I looked, sinews appeared upon them, flesh covered them and they were overlaid with skin . . . breath came into them; they came to life and rose to their feet, a mighty host* **(Ezekiel 37:7-10)**.

It was a hope Ezekiel would not see fulfilled himself, but his was the dream that one day Jerusalem would be rebuilt and the temple filled with holy people faithfully serving Yahweh.

Meanwhile, the Jews accepted their fate and settled down in Babylon, growing food, building houses and raising children. Several did well, prospered and rose to positions of eminence. Indeed, some did so well that within two generations Jerusalem became no more than a distant memory. But others kept the hope of Ezekiel's new Jerusalem alive, constantly bending over their sacred writings and crying:

> *If I forget you, O Jerusalem,*
> *let my right hand wither away;*
> *let my tongue cling to the roof of my mouth*
> *if I do not remember you,*
> *if I do not set Jerusalem*
> *above my highest joy* **(Psalm 137:5-6)**.

Ezekiel prophesied that these dry bones would live again.

The Persians

WHEN it seemed that nothing could disturb the might of Babylon, a thunderbolt shook the ancient world in the form of Cyrus the Persian. About 550 BC, after years of squabbling and war, he managed to unite the several Iranian minor kingdoms of Media and Persia until they were strong enough to challenge Babylon. Cracks had already appeared in Babylon's power structure and Cyrus took full advantage of the weakness. By 539 BC. Babylon had opened its gates to him and the Persian Empire stretched from present-day Romania in the west to the Gulf of Oman in the east, by far the largest empire the world had ever seen. The Persians were greedy for conquest, but tolerant rulers, and welcomed by many who had suffered the more austere rule of Babylon. As the book of Nehemiah suggests, there was room for local rulers under a system of *satraps*, who were themselves subject to checks from generals and civil servants and the overall control of the king.

Linking the remote parts of the empire was a good road system, which included a Royal Road, 2,500 kilometres long, stretching from Sardis in Asia to Susa near the Persian Gulf. Money became the regular medium of exchange, and to a large extent replaced the 'payment in kind' tribute, though horses, sheep, dogs and slaves were still exacted as the empire had need. New building projects were undertaken in the great cities of the empire. Both Susa and Babylon were used as capital cities until Darius I built Parsai (Persepolis), the magnificent remains of which give ample proof of the splendour that was Persia. Fish, meat, wine and honey were all enjoyed by most people in the empire as living standards improved, and there was great interest in agriculture, forestry and waterways.

The great god of the Persians was Ahura-Mazda (or Ormuzd), who was in constant battle with the evil forces of Angra Mainyu. Ahura had no image, perhaps a reason why Yahweh, the invisible God of the Jews, was readily tolerated by the overlords of Nehemiah. Other gods were Mithras, identified with the sun, and Anahita the goddess of fertility. The cult of the Magi also flourished. These were astrologer priests of the empire who continued the rituals probably learned from the Babylonians. The word 'magic' comes from their activities.

46 Cyrus (550–530 BC)

EZEKIEL'S hope for a new beginning and a new Jerusalem received encouragement from what was happening on the political scene. The second Babylonian Empire, held together with style and panache by Nebuchadnezzar, looked less solid after his death. King, governors and priests squabbled among themselves and cracks began to appear in the seemingly monolithic empire. This decline coincided with the meteoric rise of Cyrus the Persian.

Cyrus was the founder of the first 'world state' which stretched from the Aegean Sea to India. He was a wise man, tolerant and well loved by the Persians who called him 'father'. Legends surround his birth, similar to those surrounding the birth of Moses, but what is certain is that he rose from semi-obscurity to control the empire of Media and dominate the Iranian tribes on the Iranian plateau. From this base he moved west and conquered Greek city-states before turning his attention to Babylon. Here, the empire was in such disarray that even the priests of Marduk had turned against Nabonidus the king. The conquest was immediate and total, and the greatest city in the ancient world fell to the Persians—or rather opened its gates to them—in October 539 BC.

An account of Cyrus's Babylonian conquest has been preserved on a clay barrel. It criticises King Nabonidus for ignoring their god Marduk and for his policy of using slave labour. An interesting sentence for biblical scholars reads:

An account of Cyrus's Babylonian conquest has been preserved on a clay barrel.

May all the gods whom I have resettled in their sacred cities ask Bel and Nebo daily for a long life for me.

Cyrus was quick to learn from conquered people and he tolerated other customs and religions. He gained such a reputation for honour and magnanimity that the Greek historian Xenophon chose Cyrus as the model to follow when he outlined the virtues of true leadership.

According to Herodotus, another Greek historian, Cyrus was killed by a female ruler of nomads called Massagetai, in the year 529 BC.

47 Isaiah II (540–520 BC)

Isaiah 40–55

*It is sure and certain that if we persevere—and we shall persevere—we shall come through these dark and dangerous valleys into a sunlight broader and more genial, and more lasting, than mankind has ever known.**

So said Winston Churchill at the height of the Second World War. They are words that express the sentiments of an unidentified prophet who lived through the latter part of the Babylonian Exile. His words are found in chapters 40–55 of the prophecy of Isaiah, and for that reason scholars usually refer to him as second or deutero-Isaiah.

He is the prophet of hope, renewal and good news.

Comfort, comfort my people;
—it is the voice of your God;
speak tenderly to Jerusalem
and tell her this,
that she has fulfilled her term of bondage,
that her penalty is paid;
. . .
Prepare a road for Yahweh through the wilderness
clear a highway across the desert for our God **(Isaiah 40:1-3).**

From first word to last the prophet offers assurance that horror and homelessness are over and the future is bright with promise. Yahweh is about to lead a new exodus through the wilderness to their homeland.

The broad sweep of the prophet's thought is extraordinary in its magnitude. In the prophetic tradition he repeats that Israel is a chosen people.

I, Yahweh, have called you with righteous purpose
and taken you by the hand;

* From a speech made on Leeds Town Hall steps, May 16th, 1942.

I have formed you, and appointed you
to be a light to all peoples,
a beacon for the nations,
to open eyes that are blind,
to bring captives out of prison,
out of dungeons where they lie in darkness **(Isaiah 42:6-7)**.

Yahweh is more than Israel's redeemer, however He is also the arch-creator, the one who 'stretches out the skies like a curtain' and 'spreads them out like a tent to live in'. Isaiah II begins to make explicit the belief in One God which is implicit in his predecessors.

Yahweh, the everlasting God, creator of the wide world,
grows neither weary nor faint . . . **(Isaiah 40:28)**

He it was:

who made the earth and fashioned it
and himself fixed it fast . . . **(Isaiah 45:18)**

Compared with this mighty concept, how pathetic are the gods of other nations who are shaped by men. With mocking scorn he says:

. . . he chooses an ilex or an oak to raise a stout tree for himself in the forest. It becomes fuel for his fire: some of it he takes and warms himself, some he kindles and bakes bread on it, and some he makes into a god and prostrates himself, shaping it into an idol and bowing down before it **(Isaiah 44:14-15)**.

These are the gods that have been laboriously carried into exile, loaded onto beasts and cattle: 'a burden for the weary creatures'. Yahweh, on the other hand, will carry his people and take them back home to Zion. The instrument of his purpose is none other than Cyrus the Persian. He is the Messiah, the anointed one, being used by Yahweh to accomplish his historical purpose, and it is Cyrus who will allow Jerusalem to be rebuilt and the foundations of the temple to be relaid.

The prophet's confidence was not misplaced, because Cyrus did allow captive peoples, including the Jews, to return to their homeland. Furthermore, he supported the rebuilding of Jerusalem with money from the Persian treasury and returned the sacred vessels removed from the temple as plunder by Nebuchadnezzar. The famous Cyrus cylinder says that the god Marduk selected Cyrus to be 'ruler of the world', but to faithful Jews there was no doubt that the Persian was instructed by Yahweh.

This is the word of Cyrus king of Persia: Yahweh . . . has given me all the kingdoms of the earth, and he himself has charged me to build him a house at Jerusalem in Judah **(Ezra 1:2)**.

So Israel would be free. They would enter Zion with shouts of triumph and joy. Rebuilding would be rapid as more and more exiles flocked home. Soon national life would be re-organised and the resettled Jews would be ready to fulfil their destiny as 'light to the nations'.

What kind of light, though? In answering this question, Isaiah II introduces ideas so original and profound that it is doubtful if the depths of his thought can ever really be mined. Israel is to be 'a light to the nations' because she will be a servant of the nations. The longing for national pride and recognition will be attained when Israel accepts the role Yahweh has assigned to her. In five poems the prophet shows that Israel has been summoned from afar to live as the 'ideal' righteous state. Yahweh's spirit will ensure that justice reigns supreme, and from Israel's blueprint the rest of mankind will learn. In the past Israel has been despised by the nations.

tormented and humbled by suffering;
we despised him, we held him of no account,
a thing from which men turn away their eyes **(Isaiah 53:3)**.

Yet servant Israel's suffering had a redemptive purpose, for it was through the nation's anguish that lessons had been learned for the whole of mankind.

. . . Yahweh laid upon him
the guilt of us all **(Isaiah 53:6)**.

The secret of future peace and nobility lay in service rather than glory, and in righteousness rather than power. Israel was to be the first nation to realise through her suffering that:

There is no higher religion than human service. No greater creed than to work for the common good **(Thomas Paine, *The Rights of Man*)**.

The nameless prophet of the Exile had twisted the saga of Israel's history into a strange new shape which resembled a crown of thorns. It was hard to understand and harder still to live out.

48 Sheshbazzar and Zerubbabel (520–515 BC)

Ezra 1; 3; 4:1-4; 5

THE edict of Cyrus allowing foreigners to return to their homeland did not start a stampede across the desert. Many Jews had made good lives for themselves in Babylon, and of course the younger ones had been born there and had no great compulsion to return to Jerusalem. Moreover, religious views had an increased awareness of the universal authority of God and no longer saw him trapped inside Jerusalem or even within the land of Israel. He could be worshipped wherever people turned to Him, so why return to a barren land and a ruined city?

Nevertheless, a patriotic party of pioneers, led by Sheshbazzar, the son of the exiled king Jehoiachin, did return to Jerusalem. So once again a descendant of David led the Israelites. He brought back sacred vessels to the city and laid the foundation stone of a new temple. This was the first of several waves of immigrants who returned and set about rebuilding Judah's national life.

Sheshbazzar soon disappeared from the scene to be replaced by another descendant of David, called Zerubbabel. With the help of the high-priest Joshua, he set up a new altar to the God of Israel and almost immediately celebrated the Feast of Tabernacles, which was a mixture of harvest celebrations and a remembrance of the way the nomadic Israelites had lived in booths or tents following the exodus from Egypt. To this day, Jewish families still erect tents in synagogues, gardens and homes at Tabernacles.

Priests and Levites were organised to control worship and a firm foundation was laid for the new temple.

> *All the people raised a great shout of praise to Yahweh because the foundation of the house of Yahweh had been laid. But many of the priests and Levites and heads of families, who were old enough to have seen the former house, wept and wailed aloud . . .*
> **(Ezra 3:12)**

As rebuilding gathered momentum, help was offered from neighbours such as the Samaritans, but this help was curtly refused with the words:

> *'The house which we are building for our God is no concern of yours. We alone will build it for Yahweh the God of Israel, as his majesty Cyrus . . . commanded us.'* **(Ezra 4:3)**

So, as Bernhard Anderson* said, 'The hand of friendship curled into a fist' and enmity became the natural condition of Jews and Samaritans. Rebuilding plans were interrupted by hostilities, and plans to rebuild the temple were shelved for eighteen years.

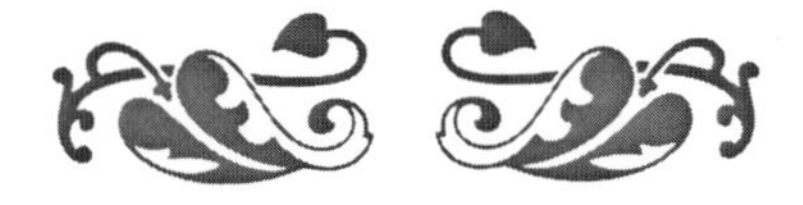

* *The Living World of the Old Testament* (Hemel Hempstead: Prentice-Hall, 1966).

49 Haggai and Zechariah (520–510 BC)

Haggai 1–2; Zechariah 1–4; 6:1-8; 8:1-8; 9:9-10

AFTER eighteen years the prophets Haggai and Zechariah stirred up enthusiasm for rebuilding the temple. The first priority of the returning Jews had been to put roofs over their heads. That had been achieved, but now Haggai believed that poor harvest and little prosperity were proof that Yahweh was displeased with the lethargy towards rebuilding the temple.

> *Is it a time for you to live in your well-roofed houses, while this house lies in ruins?... Consider your way of life. You have sown much but reaped little; you eat but never as much as you wish, you drink but never more than you need, you are clothed but never warm, and the labourer puts his wages into a purse with a hole in it* **(Haggai 1:4-6)**.

Central to Haggai's preaching are Zerubbabel and the high-priest Joshua. It is their divinely appointed task to oversee the rebuilding and regenerate the nation's life. Perhaps the prophet also hoped for national independence as well, for Darius, now ruling the Persian Empire, was struggling to quell riots which were disrupting large areas of his kingdom after the madness and suicide of his predecessor Cambyses. Zerubbabel was to be the Messiah, or chosen one, who would restore the glory of Israel.

Zechariah also has great hopes for Zerubbabel, though it is apparent from his prophecy that Joshua was struggling to maintain his position as high-priest, now that descendants of the Zadokite priesthood had returned from Babylon. Zechariah supports Joshua believing that the alliance of church and state can assure a bright future. Zerubbabel is the branch that will bear much fruit.

> *Here is a man named the Branch; he will shoot up from the ground where he is and will build the temple of Yahweh. It is he who will*

build the temple of Yahweh, he who will assume royal dignity, will be seated on his throne and govern, with a priest at his right side, and concord shall prevail between them **(Zechariah 6:12-13)**.

Zechariah's prophecies are word-pictures, many of them confusing and bizarre, but his overall message is clear. The future is bright if unity is achieved and Yahweh's place at the centre of Jewish life is confirmed. Israel is to be at peace with Zerubbabel, the man of peace as the leading figure in the restoration.

Rejoice, rejoice, daughter of Zion,
shout aloud, daughter of Jerusalem;
for see, your king is coming to you,
his cause won, his victory gained,
humble and mounted on an ass,
on a foal, the young of a she-ass **(Zechariah 9:9)**.

The first task of Zerubbabel's, to rebuild the temple, was achieved in 515 BC and temple worship was restored. Haggai at least was impressed, and ecstatically cried:

... the glory of this latter house shall surpass the glory of the former ... **(Haggai 2:9)**

In reality, it did not compare with the splendour of Solomon's temple which had been crafted by the skilled artisans of Phoenicia. Nevertheless, the modest temple became the focal point of the nation's life and the object of much devotion. Yahweh was enthroned and housed at the heart of Israel's life in Zion.

Strangely, at this juncture Zerubbabel disappears. Maybe the Persians were alarmed at the messianic expectations surrounding him and he was killed. What is clear is that there were no further attempts to revive national glory through David's line throughout the Persian period. Leadership passed to the religious sphere and the high-priestly successors of Joshua. The new Kingdom of Israel had become a kingdom of priests.

50 Nehemiah (445–433 BC)

Nehemiah 1–2; 4–6; 8–9; 12:27–13

JEWS in exile sometimes reached positions of great status within the Persian Empire. Nehemiah was such a one. He was the personal valet of Artaxerxes, the fifth of the emperors. One day when Nehemiah was at the king's winter retreat on the Persian Gulf at Susa, he had a visit from his brother and friends who had just returned from Israel. Their report of life in the homeland was depressing.

> *They told me that those still remaining in the province who had survived the captivity were facing great trouble and reproach; the wall of Jerusalem was broken down and the gates had been destroyed by fire. When I heard this news, I sat down and wept* . . . **(Nehemiah 1:3-4)**

However, Nehemiah was a man of action, and soon he had received leave of absence from Artaxerxes to return to Jerusalem and supervise reconstruction. He even acquired an escort of army officers and cavalry along with a sealed letter authorising him to be supplied with timber from the royal forests to ensure that the job was done. It was action guaranteed to provoke anger among neighbouring peoples, so Nehemiah kept his own counsel until he had thoroughly inspected the walls at night. Only when he had carefully assessed the full extent of the work did he allocate the tasks out family by family, and only when all the materials were to hand did the building begin.

At first, progress was slow and surrounding peoples such as the Samaritans, Ammonites and Arabs scoffed at their efforts.

> *. . . 'What do these feeble Jews think they are doing? . . . Can they make stones again out of heaps of rubble, and burnt at that?' Tobiah the Ammonite . . . said, 'Whatever it is they are building, if a fox climbs up their stone walls, it will break them down.'* **(Nehemiah 4:2-3)**

Undaunted, Nehemiah worked the people hard and eventually the wall was half-built. At this juncture, scoffing ceased and changed to open hostility. Plots were hatched to sabotage the work. Fully aware of these plans, Nehemiah posted guards at vulnerable parts of the wall and ordered the builders to strap swords to their sides in readiness for surprise attacks. Emergency plans were drawn up and all builders had to sleep inside the walls and be ready to fight if the trumpet sounded the alarm. Nehemiah wrote:

All the builders had to be ready to fight.

> *From that day forward half the men under me were engaged in the actual building, while the other half stood by holding their spears, shields, and bows, and wearing coats of mail . . .* **(Nehemiah 4:16)**

The strategy worked well, forcing Sanballat the Samaritan to try other methods of hindering the work. He spread rumours that the walls of Jerusalem were being built up prior to a Jewish rebellion that would place Nehemiah on the throne. When this ploy failed, they tried to coax him away from Jerusalem on the pretext of an inter-state conference, but Nehemiah would not go. Enemies inside the city tried to undermine his confidence with threats of assassination but Nehemiah was not a man to be frightened. For nearly two months, work went on day and night until all the gaps in the wall were built up and the gates replaced. Jerusalem was capable of being defended for the first time since Nebuchadnezzar's Babylonian invasion.

Having achieved the impossible in stones and mortar, Nehemiah turned his attention to rebuilding the shattered morale of the people. Former governors had bled the people dry with heavy taxes, but Nehemiah never claimed allowances due to him and by his example revived strong feelings of community spirit. He lifted the burdens of those Jews who had fallen on hard times and been forced to mortgage fields and vineyards to other Jews and sell their children into slavery. He introduced laws forbidding Jews from treating each other in this way, and got full backing from the people.

His brother Hanani was appointed to supervise the defence of Jerusalem and Levites were called from secular jobs to oversee temple functions.

For twelve eventful years Nehemiah was governor of Jerusalem, and though he returned to Artaxerxes after this time, his heart remained behind and it was not long before he was back directing operations once more. Nehemiah began to enforce Jewish laws, especially those relating to the sabbath.

> *... I saw men in Judah treading winepresses on the sabbath, collecting quantities of produce and piling it on asses ... and I protested to them about selling food on that day ... I gave orders that the gates should be shut and not opened until after the sabbath* **(Nehemiah 13:15-19).**

In seeking to foster community spirit, he made Judaism far more exclusive than it had ever been before. One could only be Jewish if one came from a recognised family with the right ancestry and if one loyally kept the Torah (law) and supported the temple. Jews who had married foreign women from Ashdod, Ammon and Moab were encouraged to divorce their wives and teach their children Hebrew. A ban on mixed marriage was imposed, even though it meant banishing people such as Joiada, the son of the high-priest.

Undoubtedly, Nehemiah's energy and enterprise had preserved Jerusalem, but his blinkered nationalism drove a firm wedge between Jew and Gentile. The great dream of a world inspired by the chosen people of Yahweh had been imprisoned in the narrow streets of Jerusalem, and Yahwehism ceased to be a crusading faith.

51 Ezra (398 BC)

Ezra 7–10; Nehemiah 8–9

THE next influential immigrant to arrive from exile was a scribe called Ezra, who had spent years studying the ancient literature of Israel. He, like Nehemiah, travelled to Jerusalem with the blessing of the Persian king and with a determination to revive Yahwehism in Judah. He carefully selected a party to accompany him which included several from the priestly tribe of Levi. They followed the fertile crescent of the Middle East in a 900-mile trek which took four months to complete. By the time they saw Jerusalem, Ezra's strategy for mission was clearly fixed in his mind.

He did not preach immediately. For two months platforms and pulpit were built in the square by the water-gate and people were 'prepared' before the mission began. When it came, all those capable of understanding gathered 'as one man' to listen to Ezra. He read from the 'book of the law of Moses', and as he read from early morning until noon, so the Levites explained the meaning in a series of sermons. The 'Mission to Jerusalem' coincided with the Feast of Tabernacles when families lived in tents for seven days in memory of Jewish forefathers who had wandered in the desert after the exodus from Egypt. It was an intense religious experience for many who were moved to tears in the fervour of revival. The

All those capable of understanding gathered to listen to Ezra.

meetings reached a climax reminiscent of Josiah's Deuteronomic Revolution, or even a modern religious crusade when the people 'got up out of their seats' and confessed their sins. On behalf of all the people, Jewish leaders signed a covenant document that bound the nation into a moral agreement with Yahweh.

Ezra had got off to a flying start, but the 'follow-up' proved more difficult. Canaanite customs, which had been the bane of previous generations, stubbornly refused to be eradicated, and some of the leaders were in no doubt where the problems lay. They told Ezra:

> *... 'The people of Israel, including priests and Levites, have not kept themselves apart from the foreign population ... They have taken women of these nations as wives for themselves and their sons, so that the holy race has become mixed with the foreign population; and the leaders and magistrates have been the chief offenders.'* **(Ezra 9:1-2)**

At this point Ezra's revival went sour and turned into an inquisition. In an attempt to rid Israel of foreign influences, husbands were encouraged to disown their wives and children, and those who refused were hounded by appointed officials. The spontaneous enthusiasm of Ezra's revival had changed into a 'night of long knives' and warm religious emotion had become cold legalism.

The touchstone for Ezra's work had been the greatness of the law of Moses, but those wonderful tenets for human living became fossilised into specialisms for lawyers. Judaism was on the way to becoming an austere religion of law instead of a life-giving spirit. Moreover, the wide vistas of Isaiah II, which had seen Judaism as 'a light to the Gentiles', had been reduced to the glimmer of a candle. Ezra had introduced a narrow exclusiveness that claimed the right to declare who were the true children of Abraham. It was a painful development which shaped the religious development of the western world.

52 Malachi (400–395 BC)

Malachi 1–4

EVEN though the modest temple had given Israel a new centre of religious activity, faith did not come easy for many. Life was a struggle for people trying to live off the land and when crops failed, God got the blame and people grumbled.

> *. . . 'It is useless to serve God; what do we gain from Yahweh by observing his rules and behaving with deference? We ourselves count the arrogant happy; it is evildoers who are successful; they have put God to the proof and come to no harm.'* **(Malachi 3:14-15)**

Malachi means 'my messenger', and whoever he was he felt obliged to take up the cause of Yahweh. He maintained that the reason blessings were being withheld from the nation was because Yahweh was despised. Although sacrifice was being offered in the new temple, the sacrifices themselves were contemptible. Instead of offering the best to Yahweh, people were bringing what they would not miss—blind sheep, scruffy pigeons, diseased and mutilated animals—while they kept the sound rams in their own flocks. They knew full well that if they offered such things to the governor he would be angry and yet they had the gall to offer them to God. Dispersed Jews in other nations offered pure gifts, but at the very heart of new Jerusalem Yahweh was being offered what the people would not eat themselves.

There was another matter that irked the prophet, and that concerned the state of Jewish marriage. He declared that mixed marriages between men and foreign women was a violation of the holiness of Yahweh, and would not be tolerated even if they poured out religious offerings. Futhermore, he was appalled at the tendency men had to divorce their wives once the flush of youth had left them. He reminded them that marriage was a covenant solemnly entered into and a wife was not something to be discarded at the first sign of wrinkles. She was a partner, a helpmate, and to discard her like a used tea bag was to overwhelm her with cruelty. The people should be under no illusion: the God of justice will come to set things right, He will take up the cause of the widow, the hired labourer, the orphan and the despised alien, and when He comes it will be as a refining and purifying fire.

> *Look, I am sending my messenger who will clear a path before me. Suddenly the Lord whom you seek will come to his temple . . .*
> **(Malachi 3:1)**

Malachi's final word is that the laws of Moses should be strictly adhered to until they witness the coming of a second Elijah—it is he who will usher in the great and terrible day of Yahweh.

53 Obadiah (390 BC)

Obadiah 1

JEWISH immigrants continued the drift back to their ancestral land. It was not an avalanche of people, but it was enough to squeeze some other settlers and cause them the same disquiet it had caused the Samaritans. Edomites had pushed into parts of southern Judea and these descendants of Esau did not accommodate returning Jews with much sympathy. It was a situation similar to that caused by twentieth-century Jews returning to Palestine, and the results were much the same.

Obadiah resented the way the Edomites had grabbed Jewish land and his little book is a tirade against the usurpers who, he believed, had rejoiced at the ransacking of Judah.

> *Do not gloat over your brother on the day of his misfortune,*
> *nor rejoice over Judah on his day of ruin;*
> *do not boast on the day of distress,*
> *nor enter my people's gates on the day of his downfall.*
> *Do not gloat over his fall on the day of his downfall*
> *nor seize his treasure on the day of his downfall* **(Obadiah 1:12-13)**.

Things are about to change; the boot will be on the other foot, because soon:

> *. . . Jacob [Israel] shall dispossess those that dispossessed them.*
> *Then shall the house of Jacob be fire,*
> *the house of Joseph flame,*
> *and the house of Esau [Edom] shall be chaff;*
> *they shall blaze through it and consume it,*
> *and the house of Esau shall have no survivor* **(Obadiah 1:17-18)**.

Obadiah is confident that Israel's good times are returning: days of fruitful gardens, flowing vines and rebuilt cities. Others may want to see Israel 'driven into the sea', but her roots will go so deep that nothing will ever move them. A distinguished Israeli called Elie Eliachar said in 1980:

> *I am well aware that if Arabs, the Palestinians and other Moslems should ever have the military power and the historical opportunity to annihilate Israel, they would do so without any qualms. For we have persistently chosen to be an alien element in the Middle East, instead of returning to our heritage as members of the Semitic family.**

In Obadiah's day choices were already being made that would result in the alienation of Israel.

* *Living with Jews* (London: Weidenfeld & Nicolson, 1983).

54 Ruth (390 BC)

Ruth 1–4

NOT everybody approved of the ruthless treatment of the foreign wives and their children. Some even had the courage to say so despite the political climate. The book of Ruth is not simply a 'Mills and Boon' love story in the middle of turgid history, but a piece of subtle propaganda on behalf of oppressed ethnic minorities.

At face value it told a tale of a Jewish couple, Elimelech and Naomi, who left Bethlehem with their two sons to seek their fortune in Moab. Sadly, things did not work out and Elimelech died, leaving Naomi to raise two sons, both of whom married Moabite women. Then, both the sons died, and Naomi, bereft and lonely, decided to return to Bethlehem, She urged her daughters-in-law to remain in Moab with their families and friends and find new husbands, but one of them, Ruth, insisted on staying with Naomi.

> *'Do not urge me to go back and desert you . . . Where you go, I will go, and where you stay, I will stay. Your people shall be my people, and your God my God. Where you die, I will die, and there I will be buried. I swear a solemn oath before Yahweh your God: nothing but death shall divide us.'* **(Ruth 1:16-17)**

So Ruth accompanied Naomi on her return to Judah.

They arrived in Bethlehem at harvest time, and Naomi arranged for Ruth to glean in the field of Boaz, a kinsman of her late husband. He was an honourable, middle-aged man, who treated Ruth with great politeness and made sure that her own and her mother-in-law's immediate needs were catered for.

But Naomi had more than charity in mind. She wanted a husband for Ruth and expected Boaz to fulfil his duty as a kinsman and make her his wife. Only after he had been placed in a thoroughly compromising position did Boaz give up his bachelor status and take Ruth to be his wife. They lived happily ever after and Ruth gave birth to a son, which gladdened the heart of Naomi in her autumn years.

> *Her neighbours gave him a name: 'Naomi has a son,' they said; 'we will call him Obed.'* **(Ruth 4:17)**

Then at the end of the story comes the punch line:

> *He [Obed] was the father of Jesse, the father of David* **(Ruth 4:17)**.

It was a well-timed rebuke of the policies of Nehemiah and Ezra, for it said clearly that David, the greatest king Israel had ever produced, was the result of a mixed marriage. Ruth, the Moabitess, was the great-grandmother of David!

55 Jonah (390 BC)

Jonah 1–4

IF Ruth was written to protest against the abuse of foreign wives, Jonah was written as a rebuke to the parochial nature of Ezra's policies, which denied to other nations the blessings Yahweh had offered to Israel. Unfortunately, so much heat has been generated in silly arguments about whether the Mediterranean Sea is capable of producing a fish large enough to swallow a man that the point of the book has been overlooked!

The Jew, Jonah, receives a commission from Yahweh to preach to Assyrian peoples in their hated capital city of Ninevah. (The volume of this hatred is clearly portrayed in the book of Nahum.) Not surprisingly, Jonah is unwilling to go and thinks he can escape Yahweh by sailing away from Israel. But Yahweh's power extends beyond Israel and causes a storm to assail the ship in which Jonah is sailing, and Jonah is thrown overboard in an attempt by the crew to assuage Yahweh's anger.

> *But Yahweh ordained that a great fish should swallow Jonah, and for three days and three nights he remained in the belly* **(Jonah 1:17)**.

Yahweh causes a storm to assail the ship.

Then Jonah is spewed out onto dry land and, lo and behold, the land is Assyria! Again the commission comes to go and preach in the city of Nineveh. This time he goes, and as he preaches, the crowds are converted in droves, and even the king strips off his robes and puts on sackcloth and ashes.

However, Jonah's preaching success brings him no joy. In fact he is furious that the loving kindness of God has been offered to Nineveh at all, for he feels that such love should be confined to Judah. In a fit of pique he sits sulking under a large plant that shelters him from the fierce heat of the day but during the night the plant withers and dies. Jonah's pique returns; he feels sorry for himself and the plant until Yahweh says to him:

> *... 'You are sorry for the gourd, though you did not have the trouble of growing it ... And should not I be sorry for the great city of Nineveh ... ?'* **(Jonah 4:10-11)**

Forget the red herring about a fish! The lesson in this parable of Jonah is that Judaism should be a missionary faith. The Jews had no more right to keep their knowledge of Yahweh to themselves than Alexander Fleming would have had to keep the discovery of penicillin to himself. If Israel's faith was worth having, it was worth sharing, for love has a broken wing if it cannot fly across the sea.

56 The Psalms

The Psalms 120–134 are especially relevant to this chapter and to pilgrims who know what it is like to journey into Jerusalem from the Mount of Olives. However, also read Psalms 8; 12; 13; 14; 22 (was this the Psalm Jesus quoted at his execution?); 23; 37; 39; 46; 70; 71; 78; 137; 139.

THE book of Psalms is sometimes called 'the hymnbook of the second temple'. It is a wonderful collection of material for use in worship, particularly temple-worship, and contains devotional verse that has nourished the spirits of Jews and Christians for thousands of years. Just as a modern hymnbook has hymns and tunes from many generations, so the psalter was collected from many eras of Jewish history. It is an anthology of spiritual experience which spans the years from King David to the Maccabees.

Music and praise were vital to Jewish worship, for Israel was a singing nation, well blessed with instrumentalists and choral singers. Leaders of choirs are sometimes mentioned in the Psalms themselves, while Levites had the responsibility of leading worship in song and prayer, ensuring that Yahweh was 'enthroned on the praises of Israel'. Many Jews lived hundreds of miles away from Jerusalem and rarely visited the temple, but when they did it was a time for rejoicing.

> *I rejoiced when they said to me,*
> *'Let us go to the house of Yahweh.'*
> *Now we stand within your gates,*
> *O Jerusalem . . .* **(Psalm 122:1-2)**.

A day in the temple was said to be better than a thousand elsewhere, and at the great festivals pilgrims came from all over the world, sharing fellowship with others along the way. The excitement rose as they approached Jerusalem. Then, at last, there she was, shimmering white in the surrounding mountains—Zion, city of God. Closely walled, the city encouraged kinship among the worshippers and was loved as Yahweh's chosen place.

As the hills enfold Jerusalem,
So Yahweh enfolds his people, now and for
evermore **(Psalm 125:2).**

Understood in a liturgical context, it is easy to see why many Psalms are arranged in parallel lines that say the same thing. The Levite would sing one line and the worshippers respond with the next:

Levite: *God has gone up with shouts of acclamation,*
People: *Yahweh has gone up with a fanfare of trumpets.*
Levite: *Praise God, praise him with psalms;*
People: *praise our king, praise him with psalms.*
. . .
Levite: *God reigns over the nations,*
People: *God is seated on his holy throne* **(Psalm 47).**

The Psalms are more than liturgy, however, they are a prayer book of meditation, confession and praise. They are proof that the highest visions of great prophets such as Amos, Jeremiah and Isaiah were not lost, but remained deposited in the life of Israel through poem and song. Like a 'prayer book of humanity' the collection is one of Israel's greatest gifts to the world. Through all the ups and downs of their experience, Israel kept the belief that Yahweh had chosen them, and the Psalms show the depth of that faith.

57 Esther (350 BC)

Esther 1–10

THE Persian Empire lasted for over 200 years, and probably towards the end of that period the book of Esther was written. It could have been a response to rising anti-Semitism or an attempt to explain the origin of the popular feast of Purim held in February or March. There is little religious significance in the book, and Yahweh is not mentioned at all, which is the reason that it met some difficulty in being accepted as holy writ. In some ways, the story reads like a Victorian melodrama with hero, heroine and villain, and it is easy to imagine the story read in a synagogue to an accompaniment of cheers, hisses and boos.

King Ahasuerus (Xerxes I) ruled his mighty Persian kingdom with an extravagance that made Solomon look like Scrooge. On one occasion he held a party for his nobles that lasted for six months! Then, at the end of that time, he threw open the doors of the royal pavilion to all men in Susa, while his wife Vashti did the same for the womenfolk. After a week's revelry, when wine flowed like the Euphrates, King Ashasuerus ordered Queen Vashti to join them and parade her royal beauty before his guests. She, obviously not keen at the prospect of being ogled at by inebriated males, refused to turn up. Ahasuerus was not pleased, especially when his advisers suggested that Vashti's action created a nasty precedent that could result in *all* Persian women flouting the authority of their husbands! Such 'endless disrespect and insolence' had to be nipped in the bud, and so Queen Vashti was removed from office.

> *. . . in order that each man might be master in his own house and control all his own womenfolk* **(Esther 1:22)**.

To fill the queen's vacant throne, a beauty contest was organised and all young virgins of the empire were encouraged to present themselves before the king. Cosmetics and finery were available by the wagonload and each girl was allowed twelve months to prepare herself. One candidate who needed little make-up was Esther, a Jewish orphan, whose guardian was a cousin called Mordecai. She kept her Jewishness secret, and in the finals she was the unanimous winner and was declared queen. Her status was firmly established, as was that of Mordecai who earned the favour of the king by uncovering a plot to assassinate him.

At this juncture enter Haman the villain, a swaggering personal secretary to Ahasuerus, and a descendant of the hated Amelekites. He was so full of his own importance that it annoyed him when Mordecai refused to grovel obsequiously before him. He determined that Mordecai had to die along with all the other Jews in the kingdom who made themselves irksome with their exclusive customs and practices.

> *Thus letters were sent by courier to all the king's provinces with orders to destroy, slay and exterminate all Jews, young and old, women and children . . .* **(Esther 3:13)**

As notice of intention, a gallows seventy-five feet high was erected on which to hang Mordecai. Throughout Susa Jews panicked, and Mordecai hurried along to see Esther and pleaded with her to speak with the king on behalf of her people. When she showed reluctance he said:

> *'. . . If you remain silent at such a time as this, relief and deliverance for the Jews will appear from another quarter, but you and your father's family will perish. Who knows whether it is not for such a time as this that you have come to royal estate?'* **(Esther 4:14)**

Esther responded to Mordecai's entreaty and waited a moment to plead her case on behalf of the Jews. At a party, arranged specifically for the king and Haman, she spelled out how cruelly her people were suffering as a result of Haman's decree. Ahasuerus was furious, and when Haman flung himself across Esther crying for mercy, he accused him of attempting to rape the queen. Haman was hustled away and hanged on the very gallows that had been built to execute Mordecai.

Haman was hanged on the very gallows that had been built to execute Mordecai.

Instead of bearing the brunt of Haman's hatred, Jews were given special privileges. Esther and Mordecai were honoured and the Feast of Purim initiated to commemorate the time when sorrow was turned to joy, and mourning into a holiday. So the story of Esther ended happily, but it raised the ugly spectre of anti-Semitism and genocide which, in the twentieth century, took the horrifying shape of a swastika.

Note: Purim comes from the word 'pur', or dice, which Haman cast to determine which day the Jews would be killed.

The Greeks

- *The later empire of Alexandar the Great stretched eastward to the Punjab and the Indian Ocean.*

THE civilisation of Greece was minute when compared to the vast Persian Empire, but its culture was irresistible and provided a foundation for the modern western world. The population of Greece probably never exceeded two million and was divided between independent city-states. Athens governed its people on democratic lines, and all male citizens would vote in the assembly and sit as jurors in the courts. Sparta was ruled by the military and imposed rigid discipline on its people who scorned easy living and prepared boys for war from the age of seven. Corinth was an oligarchy, governed by the city's leading citizens.

It was Athens that provided the stimulus for cultural advance—and what an advance it was! Philosophical debate produced original thinkers such as Socrates, Plato and Aristotle, who have continued to stretch people's minds ever since. Great political orators such as Pericles and Demosthenes dominated Athens in their day.

Pythagoras and Euclid developed principles of geometry that are timeless, and Archimedes' work with curves and spheres was a watershed in mathematics. Hippocrates is often called 'the father of medicine'. The Greeks were interested in theory rather than practice, and they never put these theories to the test in laboratories. But a man called Democritus came uncannily close to the truth in his theories on the atomic structure of matter. In short, the period of the Greeks saw an explosion of human knowledge which lifted people to new heights of understanding.

Greek gods included Zeus, Apollo and Hermes, and while they never had any sacred scripture like the Jewish Bible, they did produce great literature by the poets Homer and Hesiod, who portrayed the gods in human form and in human situations. Oracles were consulted to determine the will of the deities. Drama and sport were also features of Greek life. Sophocles, Euripides and Aeschylus wrote tragedies, while Herodotus, Thucydides and Xenophon wrote history. The Olympic Games, held to honour Zeus, included many athletic events as well as gymnastics, drama and music. Greek architecture introduced new styles, of which the Parthenon on the Acropolis of Athens is a supreme example.

Yet despite all this great understanding and learning, the city-states remained divided. They were capable of heroic action to fend off attacks from Persian kings but incapable of healing the rifts within Greece itself. Following the disastrous Peloponnesian wars between Athens and Sparta and the rebellion of Thebes, Greece slipped into anarchy and was ultimately too weak and divided to resist the advance of Philip II of Macedon, who easily crushed a last desperate alliance of Greek states. Fortunately, the treasures of Greek thought were not discarded by Philip, or his son Alexander, and were thus disseminated throughout Alexander's empire which, in the end, covered some five million square kilometres.

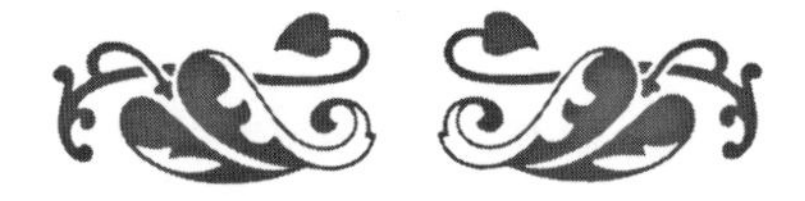

58 Alexander the Great
(356–323 BC)

THE Persians dominated the Middle East from 559 BC until 331 BC. Their leaders were enlightened and tolerant, and under them most people enjoyed peace. They were the first to spread the use of money as currency and the magnificent remains of the royal city Persepolis bears witness to the splendour that was Persia. Yet despite their fearsome strength they were never able to make serious inroads into Greece. In 490 BC Darius the Great took a great army in 600 ships to invade Athens, but as they landed on the Plain of Marathon they were attacked and defeated by the Athenian army under the generalship of Miltiades. A runner, Philipides, brought the news of victory by running the twenty-six miles from Marathon to Athens, a precedent followed by millions of Marathon runners ever since.

Xerxes hoped to succeed where his father had failed, but in 480 BC, after a victorious land battle at Thermophylae, a confrontation at sea off Salamis ended with his navy being thoroughly outmanoeuvred by the cunning Themistocles. The Persian army was stranded and destroyed at Plataea and the remains of his fleet crushed. This signalled a golden age for the democratic city-state of philosophers such as Socrates, Plato and Aristotle, of public orators such as Pericles and Demosthenes, and of writers such as Euripides and Sophocles. The additions to human understanding caused by the rise of Athens were truly phenomenal. However, the fiercely guarded independence of Greece's city-states made them vulnerable to attack, and even though Athens had achieved remarkable victories over the Persians, even she crumbled when Philip II of Macedon, using new military techniques, marched south in devastating campaigns. In 338 BC he defeated a combined army from Athens and Thebes and the whole of the Greek mainland was his. At the pinnacle of his achievement, Philip was assassinated and stepping into his shoes came his twenty-year-old son Alexander, arguably the greatest military leader in the history of civilisation.

In twelve remarkable years Alexander forged an enormous empire. He crushed rebellion in Thebes, decisively defeated the Persians in great battles at Granicus, Issus and Tyre before sacking the capital city of Persepolis. Here a huge booty was carried away on 20,000 mules and 5,000 camels. Still he marched his army onward through Afghanistan into present-day Pakistan where, after furious battles (the hardest of his career), he overcame the well-trained armies of the Indians. Legend says Alexander stood weeping by the banks of the Indus river because he had run out of territories to conquer. The truth is less colourful. His empire stretched north to the Danube and present-day Romania, south to Egypt and west to the Indus and Pakistan. Alexander might have been eager to press on, but his army was worn out and battle-weary and he had no alternative but to turn back. Marching in great heat, or often at night and on poor rations, the army limped back through Babylon. Here the great Alexander fell ill and on the 13th of June, 323 BC, he died. He was just thirty-two years old.

Alexander was more than a conquering hero. He was a cultured man who had been taught by the great Aristotle and he saw it as his divinely appointed mission to spread Greek culture and lift 'poorer civilisations' to a higher level. Soon the Greek language had spread through the conquered regions, and Greek passions such as athletics, sport, theatre, philosophy and religion had become popular. Alexander's dream of 'one world' edified and unified by a supreme culture was not achieved in his brief lifetime. Nevertheless, he had set in motion an irresistible swing towards the Greek way of life, which is usually called 'Hellenisation' after Hellas, the ancient name for Greece. The city of Alexandria in Egypt, with its magnificent library and museums, became a model for the Greek way of life, and even Jews, holding tenaciously to their ancient customs, were unable to resist entirely the powerful influence of Hellas. Athletics took place in Jerusalem itself, Jews learned Greek, and eventually the sacred scriptures were translated into that language. Just as the twentieth-century world has been unable to avoid Americanisation, so the ancient world could not withstand Hellenisation. It was an inexorable process which continued long after Alexander's death, when his formidable empire was divided between his generals.

59 Wisdom Literature
(Proverbs, Song of Songs, Ecclesiastes)

1 Kings 3:4-28; Proverbs 2–7; 10–15; 17–22; 30–31; Song of Songs 5; Ecclesiastes 1–3:15; 6:7-12; 12

THE surge of Hellenism was probably the catalyst that prompted the gathering of Hebrew Wisdom Literature, contained mainly in Proverbs, Ecclesiastes and Job. This literature, unlike anything else in the Old Testament, does not deal with the great themes of Israel's saga, such as the law, Yahweh's covenant with the nation, Israel's election, or her worship. Instead it deals with universal advice for the young, and grapples with the problems of human misery and suffering. The collection of wisdom was late, but its roots go back a long way.

In Israel the counsels of the wise were honoured alongside the law and the prophets; indeed it was said that people came to King David's counsellor Ahithophel, as they 'might make an enquiry of the word of God'. Wise men told fables and solved riddles and wise women sought to influence kings, soldiers and prophets alike.

Strangely the Wisdom Literature was dedicated to Solomon, the king whose extravagances led to the fracturing of united Israel. Stories were told of the king's own wisdom. The most famous was the story of the two prostitutes who came to the king claiming that the same baby was their son. He decreed that the baby be cut in two and each woman be given half. When one woman offered to surrender the baby Solomon declared her to be the true mother and the child was given to her.

> *When Israel heard the judgment which the king had given, they all stood in awe of him; for they saw that he had the wisdom of God within him . . .* **(1 Kings 3:28)**

The historian claimed that Solomon wrote 3,000 proverbs and 1,005 songs.

The Proverbs are often brilliant capsules of wit.

Better a dry crust and concord with it
than a house full of feasting and strife **(Proverbs 17:1).**

Bread got by fraud tastes good,
but afterwards it fills the mouth with grit **(Proverbs 20:17).**

Like a gold ring in a pig's snout
is a beautiful woman without good sense **(Proverbs 11:22).**

Others are the reflections of Agur, son of Jakeh, while Lemuel's contribution is a loving tribute to his wife whose worth 'is far beyond coral' (Proverbs 31:10).

The proverbs are not usually religious in the narrow sense, but some do equate righteousness and the fear of Yahweh with wisdom.

Do what is right and just;
that is more pleasing to Yahweh than sacrifice **(Proverbs 21:3).**

Rich and poor have this in common:
Yahweh made them both **(Proverbs 22:2).**

Proverbs are a fascinating compendium of aphorisms indicating the snares that lie in things such as laziness, drunkenness, prostitutes, fraud and nagging wives, but showing also that the basis for a good life is faith in Yahweh.

The Song of Songs is literature that seems oddly out of place in the Old Testament, where books were supposed to be ancient and religious. It has no mention of Yahweh, does not deal with any Jewish religious problem and contains no word of prayer or praise. For this reason the book has sometimes been interpreted allegorically, that is to say the woman in the song represents Israel or the Church and the man represents God. But this is not a very satisfying interpretation.

Taken at its face value, Song of Songs is love poetry and is the only book resembling erotic literature in the Bible. It reads like a collection, though one theory suggests a dramatic love poem by a woman in Solomon's harem who longs for her shepherd lover. It was nearly omitted from the Old Testament by a Rabbi council that met at Jamnia in 90 AD to determine which books were holy writ.

Ecclesiastes was another book almost left out, and its gloomy tone would seem to be the reason why. It is the homily of an old philosopher for whom existence consists of the same cycle of events continued without form or meaning. There is:

a time to be born and a time to die;
a time to plant and a time to uproot;

. . .

a time to weep and a time to laugh . . . **(Ecclesiastes 3:2-4)**

In the end, however, 'everything was emptiness and chasing the wind, of no profit under the sun'. His advice is simple enough: live the best life you can because you are a long time dead! Whoever the philosopher was, his faith in God seems distant and vague, with none of the certainty of the prophets from former years.

As the culture of Greece seeped into Jewish life, so the scepticisms of some of their philosophers was embraced as well. It was all too much for one Jewish editor who seems to advise taking the preacher's words with a pinch of salt, for he comments:

> *. . . the use of books is endless, and much study is wearisome* **(Ecclesiastes 12:12)**.

60 Job

Job 1–2:13; 42:7-17 (prose passages); three discussions: 3–14; 15–21; 22–31; Elihu intervenes: 32–37; Yahweh intervenes: 38–42:1-6

IN Albert Camus' *L'Etranger* (*The Outsider*), a condemned man is visited in his cell by a chaplain who seeks to bring the solace of God to his last hours. He listens for a while but then says:

> *Something seemed to break inside me and I started yelling at the top of my voice. I hurled insults at him, I told him not to waste his rotten prayers on me . . . He seemed so cocksure, you see. And yet none of his certainties was worth one strand of a woman's hair. Living as he did, like a corpse, he couldn't even be sure of being alive.*

That is very like the outburst wrung from Job, the hero of the finest of Israel's Wisdom Literature, for Job too refused to be fobbed off with cliché-ridden answers to the questions that racked his soul.

Job, a legendary righteous man, is mentioned in Ezekiel (Ezekiel 14:14). The book called after him is poetry with a prose introduction and epilogue. The poetry and prose give us completely different pictures of the character of Job.

The prose picture is the one that most people remember. Yahweh allows an adversary called 'the Satan' to leave the heavenly council in order to test the faith of Job. This blameless man responds to the 'slings and arrows of outrageous fortune' with a phlegmatic patience that none of Satan's barbs can do anything to disturb. He loses his possessions and his children while he himself falls victim to dreadful running sores. Yet throughout his ordeal he can still say:

> *Yahweh gives and Yahweh takes away;*
> *blessed be the name of Yahweh* **(Job 1:21)**.

Job's faith and patience endure and in the prose epilogue he is rewarded by becoming twice as prosperous as he was before.

The poetry, however, knows nothing of such fortitude. When disasters strike Job, his friends come to sympathise, but misfortune has changed him so much that they hardly recognise him. He cries out in his anguish:

Perish the day when I was born
and the night which said, 'A man is conceived'!
. . .
Why should a man be born to wander blindly,
hedged in by God on every side? **(Job 3:3-23)**

Misfortune has changed him so much that they hardly recognise him.

Faced with such blasphemous cries, his friends, Eliphaz, Bildad and Zophar, rebuke him with the orthodox wisdom of the day. Eliphaz declares:

Happy the man whom God rebukes!
therefore do not reject the discipline of the Almighty.
For, though he wounds, he will bind up;
the hands that smite will heal **(Job 5:17-18)**.

Bildad claims that it is the wicked whose light is extinguished, and Zophar asks, 'Are you to talk nonsense and no one rebuke you?' But Job will not be silenced and declares that God is so unconcerned by his agony that he does not even answer one question in a thousand; the Almighty passes by and does not even notice Job's problems and is deaf to his pleas. He simply:

. . . bears hard upon me for a trifle
and rains blows on me without cause . . . **(Job 9:17)**

Job's friends grow even more irritated by his impassioned cries and Eliphaz accuses him of being 'a bellyful of wind'. To and fro the argument goes with Job's friends repeating theological formulas and Job proclaiming that his suffering is undeserved.

God forbid that I should allow you to be right;
till death, I will not abandon my claim to innocence **(Job 27:5)**.

Finally, in frustration Job flings out a challenge to God.

> *Let the Almighty state his case against me!*
>
> . . .
>
> *I would plead the whole record of my life*
> *and present that in court as my defence* **(Job 31:35-37)**.

Argument is over, and Yahweh himself intervenes by speaking directly to Job. At last religion has become experience rather than talk, and Job confesses that previously:

> *I knew of thee only by report,*
> *but now I see thee with my own eyes* **(Job 42:5)**.

The philosophical answer to suffering remains unresolved, but Job's new relationship with God becomes the beginning of his wisdom. Job is the full flowering of Hebrew Wisdom Literature, for he represents all those who ever cried out, 'Why has this happened to me?' and wondered if life was, after all, 'a tale told by an idiot'.

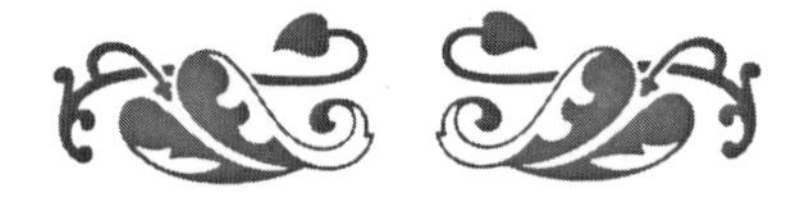

61 Antiochus Epiphanes (175–163 BC)

Apocrypha: 1 Maccabees 1:11-15, 54; 2 Maccabees 4–5; see also Daniel 9:27; Mark 13:14

THE Greek spirit continued to influence and shape urban life in Judea, even after Alexander's empire had been carved up by his generals. The eastern regions were divided between Seleucus, who held Mesopatamia and Syria, and Ptolemy, who controlled Egypt. They became bitter rivals, so once again Israel found herself a buffer state between belligerent forces. Fortunately, the Ptolemies dominated Israel for 125 years, and under their patronising regime the Jews enjoyed complete freedom of worship. Ptolemy III even visited Jerusalem on one occasion and joined in Jewish celebrations by entering the temple area with a thank offering.

Many Jews welcomed Greek culture and did not regard it as a threat to their traditional faith. A gymnasium was built in the heart of Jerusalem and young Jews took part in the games, exercising in the nude as the Greek custom was. Some even tried to remove their mark of circumcision by surgery. They were impressed by the great new learning symbolised by the Egyptian city of Alexandria, with its famous schools, museum and libraries. Here the mathematician Euclid and the physicist Archimedes gained their reputations. Common Greek became the *lingua franca* of the day and soon men were working to translate Hebrew literature into Greek. But not everybody welcomed the new culture. As in the past, when strict Yahwehists such as Elijah had struggled against the corroding influence of Canaanite religion, so Hellenism was resisted by some Jews who feared for the religion of their fathers. A sect, disparagingly called the 'pious ones' or the *Hasidim*, refused to join in the secular fashions of the day, shunning the popular Greek dress, avoiding gymnasiums and theatres, and placing a taboo on the use of the Greek language. Having separated themselves from these influences, they zealously gave themselves to the study of their ancient laws

(Torah) and the traditions of their people. Had the Ptolemies continued their benevolent rule, the Hasidim might have become a quaint anachronism, segregated from the mainstream of life, but a turn of political events decreed otherwise.

In 223 BC Antiochus III came to the Seleucid throne in Antioch. The struggle against the Ptolemies continued, with Antiochus gradually increasing his military strength and becoming more threatening. After twenty-five years of conflict, a decisive battle was fought at Paneas, near the shrine to the god Pan and which was later known as Caesarea Philippi. Antiochus completely defeated Ptolemy V and broke the Egyptian hold on Israel.

Life changed immediately for the Jews. Seleucid kings had illusions of divinity, and worship of Zeus, in the person of his regent emperor, became the touchstone of political loyalty. Friction was inevitable. Finding it unthinkable to compromise their faith, hundreds of Jews prepared to die for their beliefs. During the reign of Antiochus IV—more commonly known as Epiphanes or 'god manifest'—things came to a head.

Antiochus Epiphanes taxed the people heavily and then, seeking yet more revenue, he auctioned off the office of high-priest to the highest bidder. Two contenders, Jason and Menelaus, each offered substantial bribes, but when Menelaus was installed—who was not even from the high-priestly family—rioting broke out on the streets. Antiochus immediately applied the iron fist and marched to Jerusalem to ensure that his protégé remained in office. He began reprisals and killed many Jews before plundering the temple. But this was just the beginning. Furious at the stubborn resistance, he decided to wield the whip even harder. The practising of Jewish religion was forbidden; rolls of the sacred law were burnt; Jews were forced to eat unclean swine's flesh; the circumcision of infants was halted; and Sabbath observance was punishable by death. Finally, to crown his infamy, he went into the temple court and replaced the altar of burnt offering with an altar of Zeus and sacrificed swine's flesh upon it. This 'abomination of desolation' was meant to announce the once-and-for-all eradication of Judaism, the 'solution' to a thorn in his side. Antiochus Epiphanes' 'solution' was a chilling hors d'œuvre to the persistent anti-semitism that saw its worst manifestation in the twentieth century, when Heinrich Himmler's 'final solution' involved the gas chambers at Auschwitz and Belsen.

Terrible persecutions followed, with many being put to death and others being hounded from the cities by Antiochus's police, who insisted that the royal edicts should be obeyed.

62 Daniel (167–164 BC)

Daniel 1–12

THE last Old Testament book to be written was Daniel, and it is one of the least understood and most abused of biblical books. It has become a playground for a lunatic fringe of Jews and Christians who believe they can decipher hidden secrets from Daniel's cryptic visions, which, they say, point to exact dates in the future. Thus Daniel becomes a kind of Old Moore or Mother Shipton, and his book an almanac of the last things. They miss the wood for the trees.

Although he is never specifically mentioned by name, Antiochus Epiphanes dominates Daniel from the start to finish. He was determined to eradicate Judaism forever, even if it meant:

> *a land laid waste, with all its young men slain,*
> *Its women weeping, and its towns in terror.*

Daniel was an encouragement to the 'weeping women' and the 'towns in terror' just as BBC broadcasts in Europe during the Second World War were an encouragement to resistance fighters.

In a series of visions we are introduced to the Jewish sage, Daniel. At first he is in exile in Nebuchadnezzar's Babylon where he is renamed Belteshazzar. His three colleagues are renamed Shadrach, Meshach and Abed-nego. Their intelligence outshines all others and soon, like Joseph in Egypt, they put their expertise at the disposal of the king. Nebuchadnezzar has a dream which proves impossible to explain until Daniel deals with it. The dream is of a huge monster with a head of gold, chest and arms of silver, belly and thighs of bronze, legs of iron and feet of iron, mixed with clay. Daniel reveals that the gold is Nebuchadnezzar's Babylonian Empire. The silver is the Median Empire, the bronze the Persian Empire, the iron Alexander's Greek Empire, and the feet of iron and clay represent Alexander's Empire, divided between Seleucid and Ptolemy

(Daniel 2:31-49). In other words, the iron and clay feet represent the Hellenisers whom the writer deplores.

> . . . *in your vision, the iron was mixed with common clay, so shall men mix with each other by intermarriage, but such alliances shall not be stable: iron does not mix with clay* **(Daniel 2:43)**.

Then comes the encouragement—the monster was finally destroyed when a superhuman stone shattered the feet of iron and clay and brought the whole thing crashing to the floor. The stone was the Holy One of Israel!

The second story concerns the three colleagues Shadrach, Meshach and Abed-nego who refuse to worship a statue ninety-feet high, and as a result get thrown into a fiery furnace. They remain stubbornly faithful and God saves them. In the light of Antiochus Epiphanes's decree that *all* Jews must worship statues of himself, the point of this story is self-evident.

A further vision of Nebuchadnezzar concerns a magnificently luxurious tree that is hewn down by supernatural power, leaving only a pathetic stump. Daniel timorously interprets this as a warning to the king that his greatness will wither away and he himself will become so crazy that he will appear no better than an ox. The message is that even great kings stand under the judgement of God.

Next comes the story of Belshazzar's feast. He is called king though he never actually became so. One day he is having a carousal with his nobles and is drinking from the sacred vessels taken from the temple in Jerusalem. As they drink, fingers of a human hand are seen writing on the palace wall.

Fingers of a human hand are seen writing on the palace wall.

> *At this the king's mind was filled with dismay and he turned pale, he became limp in every limb and his knees knocked together* **(Daniel 5:6)**.

Daniel is called to decipher the writing which read:

> Mene, mene, tekel, u-pharsin **(Daniel 5:25)**.

His interpretation is uncompromising.

> '. . . mene: *God has numbered the days of your kingdom and brought it to an end;* tekel: *you have been weighed in the balance and found wanting;* u-pharsin: *and your kingdom has been divided and given to Medes and Persians.'* **(Daniel 5:26-29)**

As in Xenophon's Greek story, that very night Babylon fell!

Another well-known story tells of the Persian Darius throwing Daniel into a lion's pit because he looked towards Jerusalem as he worshipped his God.

Then the stories and visions become more pointed and bizarre. We are introduced to weird powerful creatures and then to a horn that has:

> *. . . eyes like the eyes of a man, and a mouth that spoke proud words* **(Daniel 7:8)**.

This horn, which caused the 'abomination of desolation',

> *. . . shall hurl defiance at the Most High and shall wear down the saints of the Most High. He shall plan to alter the customary times and law; and the saints shall be delivered into his power . . .* **(Daniel 7:25)**.

The horn also

> *. . . aspired to be as great as the Prince of the host, suppressed his regular offering and even threw down his sanctuary* **(Daniel 8:11)**.

Now we have arrived at the true ***raison d'être*** for the book of Daniel. The upstart horn (Antiochus Epiphanes) seemed all powerful maybe, but his day was short, 'a time and times and half a time' or 'two thousand, three hundred evenings and mornings', and then it would all be over. The worst would be passed and the power of God would be re-established.

Meanwhile, the prayers of Israel mounted.

> *'. . . O Lord, hear; O Lord forgive; O Lord, listen and act; for thy own sake do not delay, O God, for thy city and thy people bear thy name.'* **(Daniel 9:19)**

The moment of God's action was surely imminent; his day of ultimate victory was surely upon us. So the book of Daniel encouraged and inspired, and added its own grain of dynamite to the powder keg that required but a spark to set the land ablaze from end to end.

63 The Maccabees
(170–104 BC)

Apocrypha: 1 Maccabees 2:15-27, 42-48; 4:36-60; 13:41-63; 2 Maccabees 9–10

THE first explosion occurred in a small village called Modin, twenty miles north-west of Jerusalem in the hill-country of Judah. One day a Syrian official arrived to enforce the king's edict and oversee the offering of the sacrifice to Zeus. For some Jews the moment of truth had arrived—it was to be Zeus or Yahweh.

Mattathias Hasmon, an old priest and father of five sons, refused to sacrifice, and when he saw a Jew about to do so, he killed both him and the Syrian official. Mattathias fled into the hills around Jerusalem with his sons and began a bitter guerilla campaign against the occupying power. Soon they were joined by other zealous Jews, such as the Hasidim who gave to the struggle a deeply religious dimension. Almost overnight an array of terrorists and supporters had responded positively to the cry of Mattathias:

> *Let everybody who is zealous for the Law and stands by the covenant come out after me* **(1 Maccabees 2:27)**.

They became a formidable fighting force, passionate, but not blindly so, like the four thousand who refused to raise their weapons in defence on the Sabbath and were massacred as a result. The Syrians, who at first had not taken Mattathias's resistance seriously, soon realised that what the guerrillas lacked in arms and financial backing they made up for with ingenuity and bravery. They began to suffer a series of bloody noses.

Mattathias died in 166 BC and the leadership of the rebels passed to his son Judas who became known as 'the Maccabee' or 'the Hammerer' because he battered the heathen. Under Judas, the Maccabean revolt grew in confidence and effectiveness, until villages and towns fell to their swooping raids: first Beth-Horan, then Emmaus, then Beth-Zur. The Seleucids were in retreat, and in 165 BC Jerusalem itself enjoyed temporary liberation. In the following year the infamous Antiochus Epiphanes died. The pagan altars were destroyed and on the 25th of December, three years to the day since it had been desecrated, the temple was purified and rededicated. Under the new leadership of Judas, worship was restored, an event celebrated ever since in the Jewish festival of Hanukkah, otherwise known as the Feast of Lights. There was more fighting to come, though a free pardon was granted to the rebels and Menelaus was put to death.

Religious liberty had been achieved, and at this point the Hasidim withdrew their support from the Maccabees, Judas Maccabeus, however, was reluctant to disband his army and led raids into Ammon and Idumea followed by military expeditions into Galilee and Transjordan in efforts to liberate faithful Jews from the hands of the oppressor. Judas did not have things all his own way and suffered a bad defeat near Bethlehem when Antiochus V used elephants and cavalry against him. But even after that he still managed to wrest concessions from the king.

What had begun as a struggle for religious freedom had developed into a battle for political independence, which did not wane when Judas was slain in 160 BC and replaced by his brothers—first Jonathan and later Simon, the last of Mattathias's sons. Syria had divided against herself by this time and the strength of the Seleucids ebbed. Rival factions in Syria sought Jonathan's support, garrisons were withdrawn and Jonathan was appointed high-priest in 152 BC. Later, during Simon's leadership, Jews were relieved of their tax burden and independence was confirmed. Simon became high-priest with hereditary rights:

> *The Jews and the priests were well pleased that Simon should be their leader and high priest forever . . . and Simon accepted and consented to be high priest, captain and ruler of the Jews and priests and be protector of all* **(1 Maccabees 14:41-47)**.

Simon was assassinated by his son-in-law, but the hereditary principle continued in his son John Hyrcanus and became known as the Hasmonean line after Mattathias' family name, Hasmon. Under the Hasmoneans, the Jews were independent, with the civil, religious and political leadership fused in the high-priest. For seventy years the Hasmoneans secured an uneasy peace, during which time groups such as the Pharisees (descendants of the Hasidim) resisted Hellenism and the upper-class Sadducees encouraged it. They were also years when Israel experienced her first brushes with the steadily rising power of Rome.

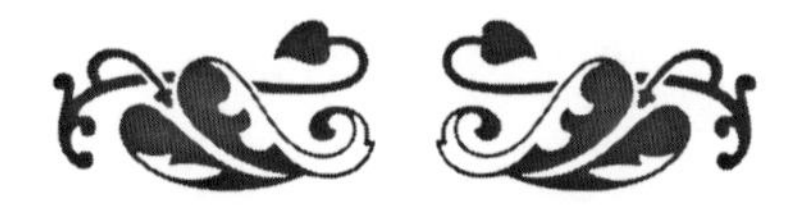

The Romans

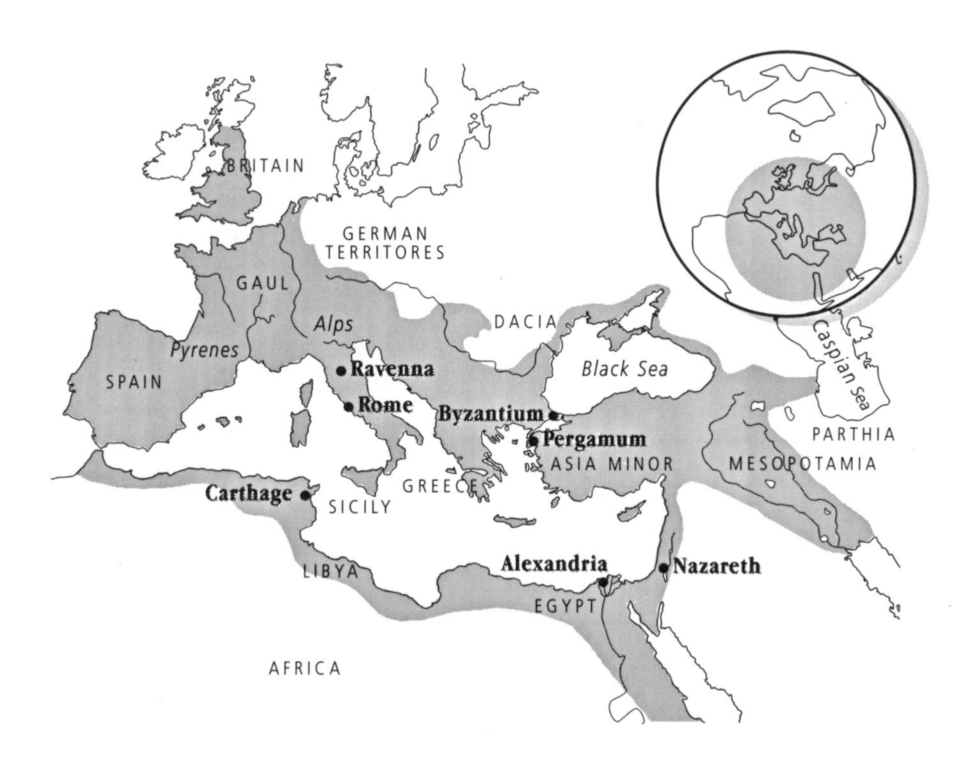
BRITAIN
GERMAN
TERRITORES
GAUL
Alps
DACIA
Pyrenes
SPAIN
Ravenna
Rome
Black Sea
Byzantium
Pergamum
ASIA MINOR
Caspian Sea
PARTHIA
MESOPOTAMIA
Carthage
SICILY
GREECE
Alexandria
Nazareth
LIBYA
EGYPT
AFRICA

ALEXANDER the Great's ideas of a world unified by Greek culture died with him, for despite the efforts of his successors the massive empire broke up into factions. Nevertheless, Greek ideas (Hellenism) lived on and many old religions and customs withered before the intellectual supremacy of Hellenism. Alexander had indicated a better way to millions of people and the world would never be the same again.

When Alexander died in 323 BC nobody could have imagined that one day a small city-state called Rome would fill the power vacuum left by Alexander. At that time Rome was busy developing farming and commerce inside the Italian peninsula with never a thought of a great empire. What drew her into international affairs was a dispute with the Phoenicians of Carthage over the grain supplies of Sicily. This dispute, usually referred to as the Punic Wars, lasted from 264–146 BC, during which time Rome grew powerful enough to develop an empire. Alexander's arm had stretched eastwards from Macedonia to India, whereas Rome dominated the western Mediterranean before spreading east to Parthia. The domination of Syria, Palestine and Egypt was not completed until Octavius defeated Mark Antony at the battle of Actium in 31 BC, after which Queen Cleopatra of Egypt committed suicide.

Rome now encircled the Mediterranean and ruled the waves. Up to this point she had been a national republic, but as power increased it became vested in fewer and fewer men, until, with the deaths of Pompey, Julius Caesar and Antony, it resided in Octavius alone. He became the first Roman Emperor, taking the title Augustus, and it was during his reign that, a decree was issued by the Emperor Augustus for a registration to be made throughout the Roman world, and a young woman travelled from Nazareth to Bethlehem to be a tick on some bureaucrat's register.

The great umbrella of Rome was now spread over a bewildering array of cultures and religions which battled for the minds of men. Some nationalistic peoples such as the Jews found strange philosophies and ideas difficult to stomach, but others soaked them up like a sponge. The philosophies of Plato, the Stoics and the Epicureans clashed with the mystery religions of Egypt and Greece, each with their adherents and brotherhoods. In the end, even Judaism was thrown into the melting pot when their sacred scriptures were translated into Greek. Ultimately, it was from this community that a sect arose that claimed to be not only the fulfilment of Jewish scripture but a hope for the whole world. How that sect outlived the fall of Jerusalem *and* the fall of Rome itself is the story of the Christian Church.

64 The Romans and Herod the Great
(100–4 BC)

Matthew 2; Luke 2

ABOUT the time Babylonia was marching Jews into exile in 597 BC, Rome was established as a city, but it took another 350 years for them to monopolise Italy. What set them off on the road to empire was the conflict with the Carthaginians of North Africa in what became known as the Punic Wars. The city-state of Carthage, in present-day Tunisia, relied on Sicily for grain supplies, and in the first war from 264–241 BC. Sicily was wrested from them by the Romans. The second war (218–201 BC) followed when Carthage defeated Spain and then trekked over the Pyranees and Alps to attack Italy, led by the famous Hannibal who was the scourge of Rome for a generation. In the third and final war (149–146 BC) Rome attacked Africa and razed Carthage to the ground.

The strain of the Punic Wars did not prevent Rome securing footholds elsewhere, and on one occasion Greeks appealed for help to free them from Macedonian domination. Romans were greatly influenced by Greek culture, to which they added their superior practical ability, especially in government and engineering.

In her earliest years, Rome was a republic, though the rich and poor were clearly divided into upper and lower classes called partricians and plebeians. Tribunes espoused the cause of the poor and did secure for them the right to become senators and consuls, though in practice this meant little because political work was unpaid and therefore remained the province of the wealthy.

At the time when the Jews were enjoying political independence under the Hasmoneans following the Maccabean revolt, Rome was going through a turmoil of riots and civil war, which eventually led to military dictators gaining control. Julius Caesar was the last of these, and after him came Octavius who took the title Augustus and became the first of over eighty emperors.

Jewish independence, secured by the Maccabees, lasted for almost eighty years, but when squabbles broke out over the succession to the high priesthood, a fateful decision was made to seek the aid of the Roman general Pompey. In 63 BC this great soldier arrived in Jerusalem and stormed the temple. He marched into the Holy of Holies, where only the high-priest should go, looking for the Jewish God, and found it empty. Pompey did not vandalise the temple, but Israel had succumbed to Roman control and her independence was at an end.

One man who benefited from Roman rule was the Idumean, Herod. He won the confidence of the Romans, as his father Antipater had done, and during the turbulence of Rome's civil war at the close of the republican period, he managed to stay in favour with a succession of Roman leaders. These included Mark Antony and Octavius, both of whom pronounced him 'King of Palestine'. Herod's rise to power was accompanied by much bloodshed and signalled the end of the Maccabean dynasty. Not surprisingly, Jews in Judah and Galilee hated Herod passionately, not least because he was Idumean, a descendant of the Edomites (the offspring of Esau) and therefore not a Jew at all. Even a friend described him as 'a master of dissimulation and consummate cunning'.

Nevertheless, Herod's achievements were considerable. Despite the hostility of Mark Antony's paramour, Cleopatra, Herod maintained the Roman's friendship and secured peace for Israel. Then, when Antony was defeated at Actium by Octavius, he proved equally useful to him and maintained his position as master of most of Palestine. Once secure, he embarked on a building programme, the magnificence of which has only recently become evident through modern archaeology. He made Jerusalem the finest city in the East and rebuilt the temple in such a way that it became the talk of the world. Ironically the western wall of that temple, the Wailing Wall, still stands today and is the holiest shrine of the Jewish world, revered as the last relic of the last temple. Building started in 20 BC and continued for eighty-four years! Herod also built Caesarea on the Mediterranean coast, naming it after Augustus Caesar and employing skilled architects and engineers to construct one of the most beautiful cities in the Roman Empire. It was full of palaces, a hippodrome, an amphitheatre, marble temple and an ingenious artificial harbour where great ships could dock safely. He fortified the great rock at Masada in the wilderness of Judah, near the western shore of the Dead Sea. This was a remarkable fortress, 2,000 feet above the Dead Sea, embellished for use as a residence to protect himself from the Jews, should they try to depose him. Masada was destined to play a tragic part in later Jewish history. Herodium was yet another of Herod's enterprises. Built five miles east of Bethlehem, it was a fortified palace on a hill resembling a volcano, with exquisite buildings inside the lip at the summit. It had terraced gardens, pools, and 200 steps of white marble leading to the citadel at the top. It was at Herodium that Herod was buried in a gold coffin studded with precious stones.

Herod was an ardent Helleniser, paying lip service to Jewish customs but promoting Greek culture as ardently as Antiochus Epiphanes had ever done. He avoided putting his image on coins out of respect for the Jewish abhorrence of image worshippers, but brought Greek and Roman games to Jerusalem itself and built temples to foreign gods. He was a cruel man, often crucifying or burning miscreants; he taxed the people oppressively to support his building programmes; he was jealous and more suspicious than Othello, murdering his own children, and beloved wife Mariamne, in periods of depression.

This was the man who sat on the throne of Israel when John the Baptist was born to an aged priest and his wife in the uplands of Judah.

65 John the Baptist (27–29 AD)

Malachi 4:4-6; Matthew 3:1-7; 14:1-12; Mark 1:1-11; 6:14-29; Luke 1:5-25; 3:1-20; 7:18-35; John 1:15-34

HEROD the Great died shortly after John was born, and when his kingdom was divided between three of his sons, riots broke out in Judea. A Roman governor called Varus was sent to quell the riots and make sure that Herod's will was executed according to the command of Emperor Octavius Augustus. **Herod Archelaus** was given control of Judea and made such a mess of the job that he was replaced after ten years by Roman procurators who took up residence in the fortress of Antonia. This overlooked the temple precincts and was a constant reminder to the Jews that Israel was again an occupied land. **Herod Philip** governed a region north-east of Lake Galilee into the Golan Heights. His subjects were largely Gentile and caused little trouble. **Herod Antipas**'s jurisdiction covered Galilee and Peraea in present-day Jordan. He survived for over forty years, but was never popular, especially with the rebel John the Baptist.

Under Rome, Israel was a seething land. Nationalist freedom fighters refused to recognise Roman authority and formed themselves into terrorist groups called **Zealots**. To them a good Roman was a dead Roman.

One religious group called Essenes, formed during the Maccabee period, gradually withdrew from public life and settled in communities beside the Dead Sea and in Judean villages. About 4,000 strong, they lived in obedience to an elected head, like Jesuits do today, but they too were intensely nationalistic and avidly studied the sacred laws of Israel. They were under training for at least three years, joined in symbolic washing rituals and devoted their money to a common fund. They sent gifts to the temple but did not make animal sacrifices. They were celibate and isolationist. It was this group that produced the famous Dead Sea Scrolls found at Qumran in 1947.

Another religious group, faithful to the Torah, preferred to stay in the mainstream of life, working out their beliefs there. They were the **Pharisees**, the spiritual offspring of the Hasidim who had resisted Greece and Hellenisation during the Maccabean Revolt. They believed the laws of Israel (Torah) to be sacred along with many traditions that had developed since exile in Babylon. They had a moral stranglehold over many working-class families because they knew the law and interpreted it as they saw fit.

A strong conservative faction sought to preserve the status quo. They were the **Sadducees**, made up of priests and aristocracy, whose position at the head of the pecking order had been confirmed by Rome. The high-priest came from this group and therefore the Sadducees controlled temple practice as well as preserving sacred laws. They did not revere the traditions so sacred to their rivals the Pharisees.

Onto this widely divided nation John the Baptist descended like a meteor. Ascetic and uncompromising, he began preaching close to Jericho on the River Jordan, and immediately his style of preaching reminded people of the words of Israel's prophets before the exile. Some even referred to him as a reborn Elijah, a significant statement because traditions had developed that claimed that Elijah would return to usher in the 'Day of Yahweh'.

His preaching was startlingly direct. If a man had two coats, let him remember the man with none; tax collectors were commanded to be honest; soldiers were reprimanded for bullying and blackmail. But the main thrust of his preaching was that the nation needed to repent. There were no exceptions. Nobody was born into a privileged position as 'sons of Abraham'; even Pharisees were 'a viper's brood' and Herod Antipas was incestuous because of his unlawful marriage to Herodias, the wife of his half-brother. Like Elijah, John was fearless and ferocious and it was impossible to ignore him. Thousands flocked to the Jordan valley to hear this wild preacher for themselves.

Perhaps influenced by the Essenes, John demanded that a person's repentance had to be signified by his immersion in the River Jordan. This symbolic bathing, or baptism, indicated a new and cleansed life ready for the coming of the Lord, and that coming was imminent. John was the herald to announce the day.

> *'. . . A voice crying aloud in the wilderness, "Prepare a way for the Lord; clear a straight path for him."'* **(Mark 1:3)**

John's popularity with the people of the land was immense, as indicated by the Jewish historian Josephus:

> *And when everybody turned to John—for they were profoundly stirred by what he said—Herod feared that John's influence on the people might lead to an uprising* **(*Antiquities*, Book XVIII, Chap. 5)**.

John paid the price for being a popular rebel and was imprisoned at Machaerus, a Masada-like fortress on the eastern side of the Jordan, another of Herod the Great's fortifications. It was here that Herodias, sick and tired of John's rebuke, arranged for her daughter to dance for the king. She pleased him so much that he would have given her anything. The macabre prize she chose was the fearless prophet's head.

The death of John the Baptist was a shattering blow to many people's dreams, but soon they were overcoming their sadness by turning their attention to a young carpenter from Nazareth. He had been baptised by John and was now causing a stir around Lake Galilee with his teaching and cavalier attitude to the law. His name was Jesus.

John paid the price for being a popular rebel.

66 *Jesus the Teacher* *(29–330 AD)*

Matthew 4:23–7; 10; 13; Mark 4; 7:1-23; 10:1-22; Luke 4:14-30; 6; 12; 14–15; John 3:1-21; 6:30-58

GALILEE was not noted for its religious sages, but during the emperorship of Augustus it produced a remarkable man called Jesus of Nazareth, whose short life changed the world dramatically. His early life was spent working as a carpenter, a trade he had picked up from his father Joseph. Then, about the age of thirty, he closed the door of his shop for the last time and began a brief public career as an itinerant rabbi. His own strictly conservative synagogue at Nazareth was not sympathetic to his radical interpretation of the Torah, so he moved to the more liberal fishing village of Capernaum on Lake Galilee. There he started teaching. Soon the district was buzzing with excitement about him. He collected a group of followers who made strange bedfellows: fishermen, a Jewish civil servant on the Roman payroll, and at least one Zealot.

At Capernaum he started teaching.

Unlike most Rabbis, he welcomed the friendship of tax collectors, landlords, prostitutes and farm workers, and spent time eating and drinking with them. His teaching was directed at fellow-Jews, but so open was his attitude that Gentiles responded to him as well, such as the Syrian woman in Tyre:

> *She begged him to drive the spirit out of her daughter. He said to her, 'Let the children [Israel] be satisfied first; it is not fair to take the children's bread and throw it to the dogs.' 'Sir,' she answered, 'even the dogs [Gentiles] under the table eat the children's scraps.'* **(Mark 7:26-28)**

His teaching method was informal, taking incidents from daily life to illustrate his message: a farmer sowing seed, a fisherman sorting out his catch, an unfinished building, a woman losing a coin, a man throwing a party, and even a lump of salt or yeast. With great skill he introduced God into the commonplace.

Earth's crammed with heaven,
And every common bush afire with God,
But only those who see take off their shoes,
The rest sit round it and pluck blackberries!

Elizabeth Barrett Browning, *Aurora Leigh*, Book 7

As with a Pharisee, who disapproved of Jesus allowing a prostitute to massage his feet, he opened windows into people's own souls.

Jesus . . . said, 'Simon, . . . Two men were in debt to a money-lender: one owed him five hundred silver pieces, the other fifty. As neither had anything to pay with he let them both off. Now, which will love him most? Simon replied, 'I should think the one that was let off most.' 'You are right', said Jesus . . . 'You see this woman? I came to your house: you provided no water for my feet; but this woman has made my feet wet with her tears and wiped them with her hair. You gave me no kiss; but she has been kissing my feet ever since I came in. You did not anoint my head with oil; but she has anointed my feet with myrrh. And so, I tell you, her great love proves that her many sins have been forgiven; where little has been forgiven, little love is shown.' **(Luke 7:41-47)**

In true prophetic tradition, some of his teaching was in active parables: he placed a child among them, he rode a donkey into Jerusalem, he broke bread and passed it round his disciples.

Pharisees tried to trap him over his liberal attitude to the sabbath and he reminded them that the sabbath was to ***help*** men not ***enslave*** them. Zealots sought to pin him down on his attitude to the heavy taxation from Rome, and he declared:

'Pay Caesar what is due to Caesar, and pay God what is due to God.' **(Mark 12:17)**

Sadducees, seeking to ridicule Pharisee belief in resurrection, concocted a story of a woman who married seven brothers and then asked him 'whose wife will she be after resurrection?' Jesus answered by quoting from the law of Moses, the most sacred part of Sadducee scripture. And when people tried to embroil him in rabbinic arguments about divorce, fiercely contested by the contemporary rabbis

Hillel and Shammai, he revealed that his knowledge of Torah was as deep as anybody's.

Although he himself followed some of Israel's traditions, such as going to the synagogue, he showed that a blind following of custom and practice could sometimes lead to breaking the law, as when tradition compelled a man to dedicate his wealth to God even though it meant leaving elderly parents destitute. Thus in keeping tradition, the command to 'honour father and mother' was broken. Without denying the validity of law and order, he made it clear that simply avoiding theft, murder, adultery and retaliation was not enough unless relationships were infused with the healing balm of love.

It was a radical and revolutionary teaching, challenging in every syllable. For Israel it was accompanied with a clear chime of judgement. After all, Jews had claimed to be the chosen children of God for the past 1,400 years, so when were the fruits of that relationship to be seen? If Israel remained fruitless how could she avoid rejection? Must the fig-tree be barren forever? (Luke 13:6-9)

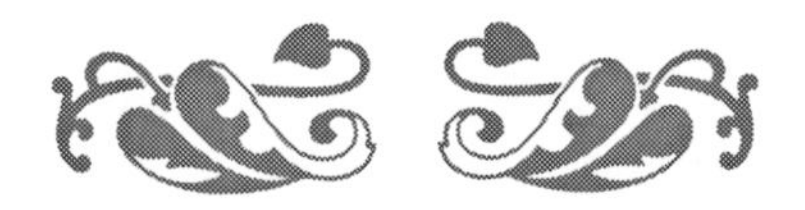

67 *Jesus: Son of Man*

Daniel 7:13-14; Matthew 26:64; Mark 8:31; 9:12, 31; 10:33, 45; 14:62; Luke 9:58; 19:10

JESUS the carpenter possessed the intuitive perception usually found in poets and painters rather than in working-class preachers. He lived out his life free from the anxiety and self-concern which plagued the fearful and defensive people around him. This enabled him to enter into compassionate fellowship with friend and foe alike, and allowed him to concentrate on the needs of others because he had nothing to hold onto himself.

He lived among people convinced that a struggle was taking place between God and Satan for domination of the world, and the message Jesus brought was that the kingdom of God was being established even during his own lifetime. He backed up his words by restoring people to wholeness: sick people were made well, thieves and rogues were converted to lives of rectitude, and warped minds were cleansed. To many, the life of Jesus was evidence that Satan's grip on the world was being loosened. Thus, when he preached about the kingdom of God he did not need to explain what he meant because it was self-evident.

> *... 'The kingdom of God is like this. A man scatters seed on the land; he goes to bed at night and gets up in the morning, and the seed sprouts and grows—how, he does not know. The ground produces a crop by itself, first the blade, then the ear, then full-grown corn in the ear; but as soon as the crop is ripe, he plies the sickle, because harvest-time has come.'* **(Mark 4:26-29)**

Later, when his followers took his message into the villages with some success, he said:

> *... 'I watched how Satan fell, like lightning, out of the sky.'* **(Luke 10:18)**

Jesus spoke and acted with authority and conviction, making devoted friends and implacable enemies. Some saw him as the long-awaited Messiah, the saviour of Israel, but others, unable to deny the power of his words and actions, accused him of being in league with the devil.

> *... 'He is possessed by Beelzebub', and, 'He drives out devils by the prince of devils.' So he called them to come forward, and spoke to them in parables: 'How can Satan drive out Satan? If a kingdom is divided against itself, that kingdom cannot stand...* **(Mark 3:22-24)**

His family became anxious for his safety and tried to persuade him to keep a low profile, but it was too late: his reputation had already spread like a bushfire and everybody wanted to hear him. Three of his closest followers became convinced that Jesus was more important for Israel than the law-giver Moses or the prophet Elijah. They believed his authority superseded anything in their ancient scriptures (Mark 9:2-8).

Jesus himself did not claim Messiahship during his preaching mission. The word 'Messiah' or 'Christ' was so loaded with political and nationalistic overtones that whenever he was in the company of fellow Jews he played down claims that were made on his behalf. Instead he referred to himself constantly as 'the Son of Man', a more nebulous title, used infrequently in Old Testament literature and the writings of the Maccabean period. As hostility towards him increased, he interpreted this title in terms of a servant whose suffering would be redemptive like that of the servant in Isaiah II.

> *'... whoever wants to be great must be your servant, and whoever wants to be first must be the willing slave of all. For even the Son of Man did not come to be served but to serve, and to give up his life as a ransom for many.'* **(Mark 10:43-45)**

Nevertheless, Jesus was uncompromising in his scathing attacks on hypocrisy and empty religiosity. So, as his fame spread, the religious and political establishment in Jerusalem began to sit up and take notice of the rabbi from Galilee. Then, when he steadfastly determined to visit the capital city for the annual Passover festival, conflict became inevitable.

68 Jesus the Martyr

Matthew 21; 26–27; Mark 11–12:1-12; 14–15; Luke 22–23; John 18–19

JESUS grew steadily disillusioned by the repressively narrow observances of Judaism. He tried to throw open windows that would allow air to freshen the stuffiness of the synagogue, but although the working classes received him gladly, the 'religious experts' and the legal profession tried to stifle him. To Jesus, these establishment figures were like trees that never bore fruit, or lights that kept their glow hidden. They were supposed to lead the people, but instead they were blind guides seeking to remove specks from people's eyes when they had great planks sticking out of their own. Such remarks did not endear him to the authorities and he became a marked man. His teaching sessions were infiltrated by spies who sought to undermine his popularity, trying to catch him with trick questions that would discredit him. They failed miserably.

Jesus decided to take the offensive and challenge the leaders of Israel at their headquarters in Jerusalem. He chose to do it at the great Passover Festival, when Jewish pilgrims from all over Israel and away from the homeland flocked to the capital to remember together the way Moses had liberated Israel from Egypt. Jesus approached the city via the steep road from Jericho until he arrived at the Mount of Olives where, three hundred feet above Jerusalem, he saw the breathtaking view across the Kidron Valley to the city itself, with Herod's

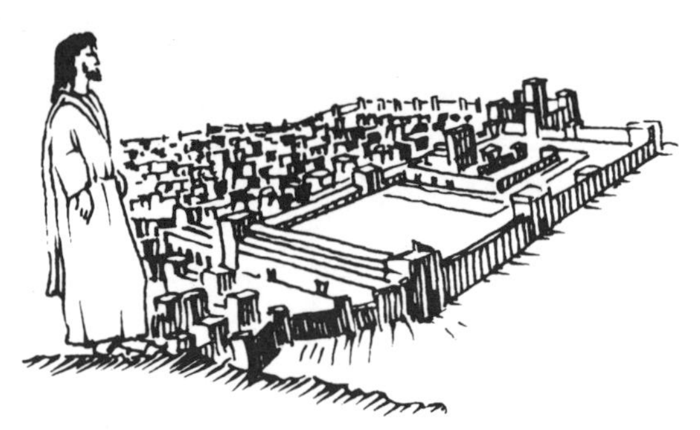

Three hundred feet above Jerusalem he saw the breathtaking view.

magnificent temple nearly complete and the Judean hills stretching away into the distance towards the Dead Sea. The sight affected him deeply and he wept.

> *'O Jerusalem, Jerusalem, the city that murders the prophets and stones the messengers sent to her! . . . Look, look! there is your temple, forsaken by God . . .'* **(Luke 13:34-35)**

Choosing his time carefully, he borrowed a donkey from a sympathiser and rode through the city gates to rapturous applause from the pilgrims, many of whom realised that he was deliberately fulfilling ancient words from the prophet Zechariah.

> *Rejoice, rejoice, daughter of Zion,*
> *. . .*
> *. . . your king is coming to you,*
> *his cause won, his victory gained,*
> *humble and mounted on an ass* **(Zechariah 9:9).**

That same evening he entered the temple precincts and watched with disgust as the priests and pilgrims haggled over the price of sacrifice and slaughtered the animals. Then he went to stay with friends in Bethany. The following day

> *. . . he went into the temple and began driving out those who bought and sold in the temple. He upset the tables of the money-changers and the seats of the dealers in pigeons; and he would not allow anyone to use the temple court as a thoroughfare for carrying goods. . . . 'Does not the scripture say "My house shall be called a house of prayer . . ."? But you have made it a robber's cave.'* **(Mark 11:15-18)**

Jesus had thrown down the gauntlet and the priests were not slow to pick it up. Obviously, Jesus' attitude to religious observance was diametrically opposed to theirs, and if Jesus was right, they were wrong. Furthermore, Jesus was treading on sensitive toes because the temple was big business and thousands of priests would be out of work if Jesus was followed too literally. It was expedient that he should be silenced quickly and quietly. Consequently, when Jesus was sharing a Passover meal with friends and followers on the Thursday night (a meal that later assumed great symbolic significance), the priests were making plans to arrest him under cover of darkness. Judas Iscariot, one of Jesus' closest followers, kept the priests informed about his whereabouts, and when Jesus moved from the meal to the Mount of Olives and the Garden of Gethsemane his activities were carefully monitored. In the quietness of the garden, he was arrested by temple police and whisked away for examination by a hurriedly convened meeting of the Jewish governing body, the Sanhedrin. A mockery of a trial ensued. Witnesses could not agree, lies were told, and eventually Caiaphas, the high-priest, claimed that Jesus had said he was the Messiah and such blasphemy deserved death.

Unfortunately for the Jewish leaders, such autonomy as they had did not stretch to the death penalty, so public executions needed to be sanctioned by Roman procurators in Jerusalem. At that time the procurator was Pontius Pilate. Roused from his bed by the priests, Pilate was reluctant to rubber-stamp the Sanhedrin request, even though the charge of 'blasphemy' had been deviously changed to 'treason' by saying that Jesus had claimed to be the 'King of the Jews', thereby threatening the overlordship of Rome. But eventually the Roman, who had a reputation for ruthlessness, gave way to expediency and signed the order for the flogging and execution of Jesus.

When the ordinary pilgrims stirred on the Friday morning and returned to the city centre, Jesus was already a condemned man and the machinery of execution was being erected by the Roman soldiers. By 9 am he was strung up outside the city wall on the crucifixion scaffold along with two insurgents. Six hours later, by the middle of the afternoon, he was dead.

Another Jewish pretender had gone the way of many others. But this one was different, for Jesus of Nazareth refused to be just one more execution statistic. His life and death would never be forgotten.

69 Peter (29–64 AD)

Mark 1:16-20, 29-34; 5:21-43; 8:27-33; 9:1-8; Luke 5:1-11; 22:24-34, 54-61; John 20:1-9; 21:1-23; Acts 2–5; 9:31–12; the two letters of Peter

DURING the brief ministry of Jesus, Peter the fisherman became one of his closest followers. A Galilean, he had thrown in his lot with Jesus from the earliest days, risking the vagaries of life with a wandering preacher, even though it meant less fishing and great insecurity for his wife and family. Peter did not always understand what Jesus was up to, but he knew that his mother-in-law had been healed by him and he had been part of the inner circle that had seen Jairus's daughter brought back from the jaws of death. He grew very close to the rabbi, who used him as a sounding board to gauge the mood of the people, and when there were decisions to make, Peter and the Zebedee brothers, James and John, were usually consulted.

It was Peter who first began to articulate the joy of what it meant to be part of the loving fraternity inspired by Jesus, and he was the first to suggest that the life of Jesus was the most important thing that had ever happened in Israel's history. To Peter, Jesus was more than a rabbi and friend, he was the hope of Israel—the Messiah. He was devastated by the malevolent opposition they experienced in Jerusalem. All the followers were shattered by the rapid events that had snatched the rabbi from them, but Peter suffered most from remorse and regret. Yet, despite the grief, the fellowship they had forged in their time with Jesus lived on and kept them together. If the 'new life' Jesus had offered them was valid while he was with them, why should it dwindle now? Why should it not go on forever?

Remarkably, the presence of Jesus came to them with renewed force—he was resurrected among them, freed from the shackles of time and space and abroad in the world. Jews who had not committed themselves to the Galilean rabbi during his life congregated together to discuss his teaching. Many followed his example of baptism and others met regularly to share a meal and pray. The truly committed ones formed themselves into a fraternity so close that they shared everything and denied the right to private ownership.

Peter, supported by John, became the recognised leader of the fellowship in Jerusalem and was bold enough to start preaching in the temple precincts. It was not long before the priests realised that in killing Jesus they had only 'scotch'd the snake, not kill'd it'. Peter preached his conviction that all Israel's years of hope found their fulfilment in Jesus. He was the one who made sense of Israel's past, from Abraham to John the Baptist, and no matter what happened to his followers, his kingdom was capable of saving men from themselves and making them truly human. Jesus was resurrected and would never die. It was preaching guaranteed to ignite powder kegs, and when this was supported by evidence of healing, the authorities resorted to imprisonment. But the message would not be chained. By now some priests had become believers, and when Peter and others were imprisoned, sympathisers let them out and back they went to preaching.

> *. . . every day they went steadily on with their teaching in the temple and in private houses, telling the good news of Jesus the Messiah* **(Acts 5:42)**.

Nothing could prevent the spread of the 'good news' and soon Peter, leaving the Jerusalem fellowship to the leadership of Jesus' brother James, was preaching to Greek-speaking Jews and Gentiles as far north as Jaffa on the Mediterranean coast. Even the Roman stronghold at Caesarea, built by Herod, was pierced by the words of Peter when Cornelius, a much-respected centurion of the Italian Cohort, invited Peter to speak to his relatives and friends. The persuasiveness of his words overwhelmed them all and they became such ardent believers that Peter baptised them into the fellowship before he left.

The baptism of Cornelius and his companions provoked the first great argument within the community. Were Gentiles to be admitted to the fellowship, even though they were not Jews and therefore uncircumcised? It was a question that concerned the fellowship for a generation as the 'good news' about Jesus took the Roman world by storm. By the time Peter was executed in the city of Rome itself, belief in Jesus the Messiah had burst asunder the confines of Judaism and was reshaping the Roman Empire.

70 Stephen and Philip (34–35 AD)

Acts 6–8

BELIEF in Jesus as Messiah spread like a prairie fire, but the believers still remained a sect within Judaism and kept up their worship at the temple. In the synagogue they passionately pleaded their case that Jesus was Messiah. The Greek-speaking synagogue also included Jesus' followers, many of whom had joined the totally committed fraternity that had sold all their possessions and contributed to a common pool. On one occasion some of these Jewish-Greek speakers (Hellenists) complained that their widows were being overlooked when the pool was being distributed and so, to scotch any rumours about favouritism, seven Hellenists were elected to administer day-to-day affairs, leaving the other apostles free to preach.

One of the administrators was called Stephen, and soon he proved to be quite a preacher in his own right. His outlook was radical and some accused him of blaspheming against Moses and God. Pious Jews brought him to the Sanhedrin and charged him with undermining the Jewish faith and claiming that in some way Jesus of Nazareth was going to destroy the temple.

Stephen defended himself by outlining Jewish history from the days of Abraham to the days when Solomon built Jerusalem's first great temple. He pointed out there was a considerable period when Jews had not had a temple and therefore it was obvious that it was not essential to faith.

> '*... the Most High does not live in houses made by men: as the prophet says, "Heaven is my throne and earth my footstool ..."*'
> **(Acts 7:48-49)**

Taking the offensive, he accused the Sanhedrin of being deaf to the truth.

> '*... Like fathers like sons. Was there ever a prophet whom your fathers did not persecute? They killed those who foretold the coming*

of the Righteous One; and now you have betrayed him and murdered him . . .' **(Acts 7:51-52)**

This speech provoked a predictable response. In a frenzy of anger they dragged him from the Council and flung him outside the city wall where they stoned him. Battered to his knees, he lifted his bloodied head in a last gesture of defiance and prayed that the Lord Jesus would forgive his murderers. Then he died. A witness to the murder was a young Greek-speaking Jew called Saul, who fully approved of Stephen's murder.

Stephen was the first follower of Jesus to die for his belief, the first of a long line of witnesses. Jewish abhorrence of the new sect gained in vehemence and Herod Agrippa, grandson of Herod the Great and friend of the Roman Emperors Gaius Caligula and Claudius, sought to ingratiate himself with the Jews by hounding members of the new sect. Peter was imprisoned and James, the brother of John, was beheaded. The wave of persecution led to many believers leaving Jerusalem for less hostile cities, and soon communities were established in Judea, Samaria, Phoenicia, Cyprus and Antioch in Syria. It was at Antioch that the sect were first nicknamed 'Christians' because they claimed that Jesus was 'Christ'.

Philip, like Stephen, one of the administrators elected by the fellowship in Jerusalem, headed for Samaria preaching throughout the countryside and conducting a successful healing mission. Hundreds responded and were baptised, including a famous magician called Simon. He was the one who later angered Peter and John when they were visiting Samaria by trying to buy the power the Christians possessed. (This incident added the word 'simony' to our language.) Philip continued his work for many years using Caesarea as his headquarters. Caesarea, with its ingenious artificial harbour, built by Herod the Great, served as the capital of the Roman government of Palestine and was a strategic place for spreading the new faith. It was Philip who explained to an Ethopian official and Jewish sympathiser that the suffering servant mentioned in second Isaiah was fulfilled in the person of Jesus. The Ethiopian was duly baptised and he might well have been the first person to take Christianity to Africa.

The persecutions of Christians gained momentum in Jerusalem, fuelled by the psychotic hatred of Saul, the Jew from Tarsus, who had been involved in Stephen's murder and now harried the believers with uncompromising ferocity. Bursting into homes, he seized men and women and sent them to prison. Incredibly, it was this ruthless inquisitor who was to become Christianity's greatest evangelist.

71 Paul the Missionary (35–64 AD)

Acts 8:1-3; 9:1-30; 13–28

SAUL the Pharisee was so zealous in his persecution of the Christian sect that he was granted permission to ferret out believers who lived 150 miles away in Damascus and bring them back to Jerusalem. The journey changed his life. It gave him time to consider the nature of his inquisition and reflect on his own dissatisfaction with Judaism. He harked back to the death of Stephen and thought about the quality of life being lived out by the new sect. Most important of all, he pondered about Jesus himself, and by the time he and his party were within sight of Damascus Jesus had become Saul's magnificent obsession. His conversion was so dramatic that it changed the direction of his life and transformed the inquisitor into an evangelist.

Saul's about-face was accompanied by a mental and physical breakdown, and though most Christians were suspicious of the new Saul, a man called Ananias nursed him back to health and welcomed him into the fellowship of the community. He withdrew to the Arabian desert for a while to think through his new faith and when he returned to Damascus it was as a compelling preacher.

> *. . . Saul grew more and more forceful, and silenced the Jews of Damascus with his cogent proofs that Jesus was the Messiah* **(Acts 9:22)**.

Saul grew more and more forceful.

Now it was Saul's turn to be a marked man, for Jews in Damascus and Jerusalem wanted his life, forcing him to seek refuge in his home town of Tarsus.

He lived there for some months until Barnabas, the uncle of Mark the gospel-writer, sought him out to help with the flood of conversions that were taking place at Antioch in Syria. They got on well and after a year decided to set off on a missionary journey in an attempt to spread Christianity into Asia. Saul now adopted the Roman name Paul, and with the blessing of the fellowship at Antioch and accompanied by John Mark, they embarked on the journey that took them to Cyprus, Pamphylia in present-day Turkey (where John deserted them), and across the Taurus Mountains to Pisidian Antioch later called Ankara. Their method was to seek out cities with Jewish communities and preach the news of Jesus to them. At a synagogue in Ankara they met hostility from the Jews, whereas Gentiles received the message warmly. They journeyed to Iconium where, after initial success with Jews and Gentiles, they were ill-treated and escaped to Lystra. Again after early successes, Jews from Ankara and Iconium stirred up opposition and Paul was stoned within an inch of his life. He recovered, so they retraced their steps before sailing back to Syria to report to the fellowship at Antioch.

> *When they arrived and had called the congregation together, they reported all that God had done through them, and how he had thrown open the gates of faith to the Gentiles* **(Acts 14:27)**.

Soon they were thinking of a second journey, but Barnabas was keen to take John Mark again and Paul was not. The argument was so fierce that Barnabas and Mark sailed to Cyprus and Paul returned to Asia with a new companion called Silas. They went through Asia encouraging the believers until they reached the western coast of Turkey and stood looking across the Dardanelles towards Europe. Here they met a doctor called Luke who persuaded them to sail to Macedonia and stay at the Roman city of Philippi. There was no synagogue here, but they preached with some success by the riverside until they were flogged and imprisoned. Nevertheless, they made friendships that endured to the end of Paul's life.

Paul and Silas were now determined to press on westward, eager to preach in northern Greek cities such as Thessalonica and Beroea. Always they stirred up opposition, but always they made converts. Then southwards Paul journeyed to Athens and Corinth, earning his own living as a tent-maker but never wasting an opportunity to say a word about Jesus. The troubles that blew up in the fellowship in Corinth nearly broke his heart, but still he pressed on—back into Asia to Ephesus, then back to Greece and Macedonia, ever travelling, ever preaching.

After years of this punishing schedule, his restless spirit urged him to return to Jerusalem despite warnings and steady opposition from hostile Jews. There he was well received by Jesus' brother James, who was now leader of the Jewish Christian believers in the the capital. Unfortunately, Paul's arrival at the temple provoked a riot and he again found himself in custody. The situation was ugly and getting out of control—one group of Jews had even taken a vow not to eat or drink until they had killed him. Paul decided to appeal to Roman justice, and as he was a Roman citizen he was despatched to Italy forthwith.

The harrowing voyage, which involved privation and shipwreck, was graphically recorded by his companion Luke, but eventually they arrived at Rome where he was kept under house-arrest for several years. He continued to write and preach to the end. Tradition says he was executed in Rome, possibly during the reign of the infamous Nero.

By that time Christianity was seeded at the very heart of the Empire and the restless endeavour of Paul, the Jew from Tarsus, had ensured that the name of Jesus would outlive the Empire itself.

72 *Paul the Thinker*

PAUL the intrepid missionary was also the outstanding thinker of the early church. He was the guiding genius responsible for planting and nurturing Jewish Christian beliefs into the alien soil of the Gentile world. He was well qualified to do so. His knowledge of Greek and Roman culture derived from his childhood in Tarsus; he was well schooled in Jewish history and tradition because of his training as a Pharisee at Jerusalem; and his experience of Christianity had come from his own dramatic conversion on the Damascus Road. He drew from a rich background, which enabled him 'to become all things to all men'.

He was far too busy to be a systematic and consistent thinker, instead working out his theories on the anvil of experience and dashing off his letters at dictation speed to a secretary. He was concerned with the doctrine of the faith but he was even more concerned with being a father to the newly-formed fellowships that grappled with the multifarious problems of living in a pagan world.

The first great question that taxed him was the nature of Christianity. Was it simply a sect of Judaism or was it something completely different? Some believed that converts who joined the fellowships should be circumcised like all good Jews, and even Paul had his young friend Timothy circumcised according to tradition. What Paul advocated, however, was that circumcision and minute adherence to Jewish law were irrelevant to the Gentile world where belief had become a matter of faith rather than legal rectitude. A Christian council was called in Jerusalem to debate this thorny issue and Paul won an argument from Jewish Christians there, led by Jesus' brother James, that circumcision should not be insisted on. However, despite a circular from this council, the argument persisted for years, leading Paul on one occasion to snatch the pen from his secretary as he copied a letter to Christians in Galatia, and write a postscript in block capitals:

> *Circumcision is nothing; uncircumcision is nothing; the only thing that counts is new creation!* **(Galatians 6:15)**

Another great problem for the Apostle was to instil into the fledgling believers the idea that God was concerned with personal morality. Therefore, when Paul heard that the Corinthian fellowship had among them a man who was involved in a sexual liaison with his step-mother, he was appalled and advised that the man should be excommunicated until he came to his senses. Other problems concerned him: a man had taken a fellow-believer before a pagan court. Some Christians were married to non-believers and some people questioned Paul's authority as an apostle because he had not been one of the original twelve disciples. In the turbulent first years of Christianity, people did not flock into the fellowships as ready-made saints but as thieves, drunkards, swindlers, homosexuals, whores and adulterers. They were the rough clay waiting to be recreated into people like Jesus.

Paul had to overcome disappointment when friends such as Demas deserted him; he worried over personal squabbles such as the one between the women Euodia and Syntyche at Philippi; and he worked to reconcile a runaway slave called Onesimus to his master Philemon. He was ever mindful of the snares waiting to trap the unwary in a garishly pagan world where sacred prostitution appeared to give the stamp of approval to licence and where it was difficult to find meat that had not been dedicated to pagan gods (Philippians 4:2; 2 Timothy 4:9; Philemon).

The fundamental message Paul delivered throughout his preaching was that the spirit of Jesus the Jew lived on in the world and was capable of infusing believers in such a way that it gave them power to live lives of purity and compassion. From his own experience, Paul declared that what the laws of Judaism could not do faith in Jesus as the Messiah had accomplished. His slavish following of the law had meant that his relationship with God had been like that of a slave to a master, whereas his faith in Christ had revealed God as his father.

In an endeavour to articulate his new-found life, Paul wrote over and over again of Christ living within him or of being a new creature in Christ. It was not something he had earned but something he had accepted because of the grace of God working within him.

This grace had transformed his life and it compelled him to preach. He was a beggar telling other poor beggars where they could find bread. Paul's thought, life and preaching were so irresistibly compelling that, more than any other evangelist, he Christianised the tired Roman Empire, and in so doing shaped the development of the western world. He bridged the enormous gap between Jewish and Gentile worlds by presenting the Jewish Messiah as the Saviour of Mankind. The irony was that as millions of Gentiles accepted this Jewish Saviour, most Jews rejected him.

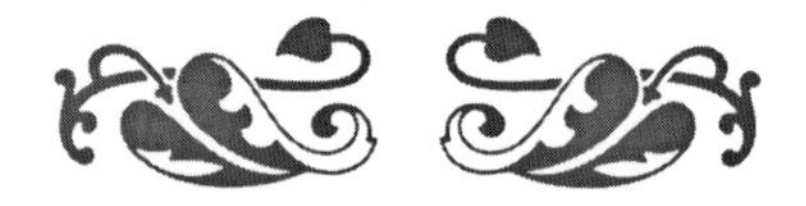

73 *John Mark*

Mark 1–16; Acts 12:11-17, 25; 15:36-41; 2 Timothy 4:11

STITCHING together facts and hints, it is possible to see John Mark growing from childhood to adolescence during the ministry of Jesus of Nazarath. Mary, his mother, was a supporter of the rabbi and her home in Jerusalem was a favourite rendezvous for his followers. Perhaps the last supper Jesus shared with his disciples was in an upper room of his very home, allowing Mark to see something of that sombre meal before he followed the group to the Mount of Olives where he witnessed the arrest of Jesus in the Garden of Gethsemane. He was probably the young man who followed that night dressed only in a linen cloth and when the temple guards grabbed him,

> *. . . he slipped out of the linen cloth and ran away naked* **(Mark 14:52)**.

A year or so later, King Herod attacked the church beheading James, the son of Zebedee, and imprisoning Peter. Then, when Peter escaped:

> *. . . he made for the house of Mary, the mother of John Mark, where a large company was at prayer. He knocked at the outer door and a maid called Rhoda came to answer it. She recognized Peter's voice and was so overjoyed that instead of opening the door she ran in and announced that Peter was standing outside. 'You are crazy', they told her; but she insisted that it was so . . . Meanwhile Peter went on knocking, and when they opened the door and saw him, they were astounded* **(Acts 12:12-16)**.

Around this time, Mark's cousin Barnabas introduced him to the apostle Paul and he accompanied them on the first missionary tour, working as an assistant. Sadly, when they landed at Perga in Asia, he lost his stomach for the job and deserted them, returning home to

Jerusalem. Later, when plans were being made for a second tour, Barnabas wanted Mark with them again, but Paul would not hear of it. The disagreement became so vehement that Paul chose a new colleague called Silas and Barnabas sailed with Mark to Cyprus. The rift with Paul was resolved in later years when Mark became a useful and close friend of the apostle during his imprisonment at Rome. Mark was also a companion of Peter, who refers to him warmly as 'my son' in his letter from Rome. The strongest church traditions tell us that Mark helped Peter by being a kind of interpreter, perhaps helping Peter express himself in Greek. The stories Peter told were remembered by Mark, and that is why so much of his gospel reads like the recollections of an eyewitness. His work has been neatly called 'the reminiscences of Jesus as told by Peter to his friend John Mark'.

Why did he write a gospel in the first place? As the years passed by, many of the original companions of Jesus passed away, a process accelerated when Emperor Nero vented his spleen on hapless Christians living in Rome, displaying a growing antagonism towards the Jews. It became a matter of some urgency that the things Jesus had done and said should be written down before they were corrupted or forgotten. And who was better qualified to do this than Mark? He was not a literary genius by any means, but he had known Jesus and he had been a close friend of both Peter and Paul. So he wrote a brief account of the life of Jesus, using as a framework the basic ingredients (the *kerygma*) of the apostles' preaching. What his work lacked in style, it made up for in raciness and passion and though his ending is very abrupt, perhaps even lost, it proved to be a very useful tool for the expanding Church. Later writers used Mark as a basis for their 'Lives of Jesus'. Laurence Housman described Mark as

> *The saint who first found grace to pen*
> *The life which was the Life of Men* (***Songs of Praise***, **No. 228**).

It was through this unscholarly and somewhat ordinary man that millions who had never known Jesus of Nazareth in the flesh got to know him in a book.

74 James the Brother of Jesus

Matthew 13:53-58; Mark 6:3; Acts 15:1-21; 21:18-26; 1 Corinthians 15:1-7; Galatians 1:18-19; James 1–5

WHEN Jesus closed the door of his carpenter's shop in Nazareth for the last time and began a new career as an itinerant rabbi, he did not sever connections with his family. They followed his movements with interest and growing alarm as antagonism from the establishment increased. On occasions they feared for his safety and sought to restrain him, but without success. We hear nothing of his brothers and sisters by name, but after the crucifixion Paul declared that Jesus' brother James was a witness to the resurrection. Thereafter he became the leader of the Jewish-Christian community in Jerusalem. He was widely respected and became the champion of Jewish Christianity because of his ascetic lifestyle and piety which earned him the title 'James the Just'.

During the dispute about whether Gentile converts should be circumcised, James took the middle position, not wanting to curb the remarkable work of Paul but wanting to cool the anger of orthodox Jews. He presided over a council of Jerusalem convened to tackle this thorny problem. On one side was Paul advocating that Gentiles should be free from the irksome restraints of Jewish laws such as circumcision, a position supported inconsistently by Peter. On the other side were the Pharisee-Christians who stated categorically that 'They must be circumcised and told to keep the Law of Moses'.

The diplomatic compromise that James came up with and which gained acceptance was that they:

> *. . . should impose no irksome restrictions on those of the Gentiles who are turning to God, but instruct them by letter to abstain from things polluted by contact with idols, from fornication, from anything that has been strangled, and from blood* **(Acts 15:19-20)**.

James was friendly with Paul, but he also maintained the respect of Jews living in Jerusalem. The letter called after his name reflects the compromise position that this brother of Jesus adopted in trying to win over the descendants of Abraham. Martin Luther called James's letter 'a right strawy epistle' because it says nothing about men being saved by their faith. But James had a point when he indicated that faith without action was useless. Every word of his letter shows him to be a reconciler, and in those early passionate and heady days of missionary zeal, the brother of Jesus had an important role to play.

However, even James could not stem the flood of hatred that eventually turned on the Christians and in the end overwhelmed James himself. He was executed by special command of the high-priest, an action that drove a final wedge between Jew and Christian. Christians fled to Pella, east of Lake Galilee, and were thereby spared the horrors about to be meted out to Jerusalem.

75 The Jewish War

Mark 13; Josephus, Jewish War, Book 7

THE Romans could never understand why the Jews stubbornly resisted the colonisation of Israel and the spread of Graeco-Roman culture. None of the procurators sent from Rome succeeded in getting alongside the people of the land, and many of them made fatal errors of judgement which increased hostilities within Israel. Pontius Pilate, for example, took money from the temple treasury to pay for the building of an aqueduct and was unable to understand why this should lead to riots in the streets. He then compounded his error by putting the riots down with force. Another mistake was to carry flags bearing the emperor's image through Jerusalem, thereby offending the religious sensitivities of the pious.

Large numbers joined armed rebellious bands such as the Zealots, and under the procurator Felix, before whom the apostle Paul was tried, assassinations became commonplace. The Romans retaliated with mass crucifixions which escalated the violence even further, and soon the revolt became organised. Remembering the way the Maccabees had won religious and political independence from the Greeks during the Maccabean Revolt, leaders sprang up who urged the Jews to believe that the same would happen with the Romans. Guerilla bands attacked cities where the Roman garrisons were weak, and parts of Israel were liberated and Jewish coinage was issued again. But when Rome, in a massive show of force, sent 60,000 of her finest troops to Israel, the end was inevitable.

Led by the general Vespasian, the troops slaughtered thousands in ghastly reprisals, and by 69 AD only Jerusalem and outlying fortresses by the Dead Sea were still in Jewish hands. The inevitable was delayed when Vespasian returned to Rome to claim the purple after the murder of Emperor Nero, but his son Titus remained to press the siege of Jerusalem. It was a dreadful time, not only because of Rome battering at the gates, but because of civil strife inside the city itself. A peace-making faction were overwhelmed by rebels who murdered them. Then the rebels fought among themselves even while the city was under attack. Thousands died of starvation and disease, and so appalling were conditions inside the walls that the living ate the flesh of the dead. After five months Jerusalem fell and was thoroughly laid to waste. The temple of Herod the Great, eighty-four years in the making and completed for only six, was virtually razed to the ground leaving only the western wall to indicate how magnificent the temple had been. Today this 'Wailing Wall' is the most sacred place in Judaism.

It was during this Jewish War that the Essene monastery of Qumran on the north-western shore of the Dead Sea was destroyed. It had been in existence for 200 years and was the home of a monastic order who shared all their possessions and purified themselves by ritual washing. They were a strict sect who objected to much that went on in Jerusalem's temple. The monastery included a large scriptorium where sacred literature was copied out, including all the Old Testament except the book of Esther. When they were attacked by the Romans they hid these sacred scrolls in the warren of caves in nearby cliffs. They remained there for nearly 1,900 years until they were discovered accidentally by a bedouin goat-herd in 1947.

The fall of Jerusalem in 70 AD ended Jewish resistance apart from that by a group of Zealots who left the city before the siege and occupied the amazing fortress of Masada. This was the flat-topped hill high above the shores of the Dead Sea which had been converted into an impregnable fortress by Herod the Great. It was equipped with huge water cisterns, grain storerooms, barracks, an arsenal

They built a massive ramp to breach the defences.

and a splendid palace. These Zealots, with their wives and children, about a thousand in all, were prepared to defy Rome to the end. In 72 AD the Roman Tenth Legion surrounded the rock, and using slave labour built a massive ramp to enable their troops to breach the defences. Masada, under the command of Eleazar Ben Yair held out for eight months. Finally, when they realised that further resistance was impossible, a solemn pact was made and the men killed their wives and children. Then, after drawing lots, ten men killed the rest and, after lots again, one man killed the remaining nine before falling on his sword. Josephus, the Jewish historian, said:

> *When they discovered the numbers of the dead, the Romans did not rejoice at the enemies' downfall, but admired the noble decision and the unwavering defiance of death of so many people* (***Jewish War***).

Jewish resistance to Rome had come to a spectacular end.

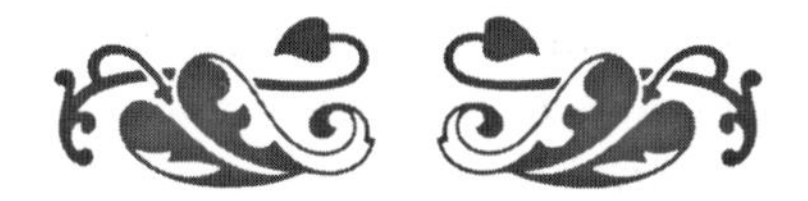

76 Matthew

Matthew 5–7; 10:9–11:1; 13; 18; 23–25; Transfiguration: 17:1-8

THE only thing one can say with certainty about Matthew is that he is numbered among the disciples of Jesus. The gospel named after him says that he was a tax collector, but Mark and Luke call the tax collector Levi. They could be the same person, of course, but that is anybody's guess.

The gospel named after Matthew was not written by the disciple of that name, otherwise he would not have relied so heavily upon Mark, ninety percent of whose gospel he repeats, much of it word for word. It remains one of the mysteries of New Testament scholarship why the name of Matthew should ever have become attached to the gospel at all. But by 110 AD this was certainly the case, and it is quoted by Bishop Ignatius of Antioch in Syria, which has led some people to suggest that the gospel was written in Syria to prove to Jews there that Jesus was the Messiah. Another suggestion is that the disciple Matthew was the author of the anthology of Jesus' sayings that we know existed from early days and was used by Luke. So what could have happened is that the compiler of this gospel used Matthew's collection of sayings and combined them with Mark's gospel and other material of his own. But the way he used these sources gives his work a flavour all of its own.

Lacking the vigorous movement of Mark, it concentrates instead on arranging the teaching of Jesus in five separate collections, each ending with the formula:

> *When Jesus had finished this discourse . . .* **(Matthew 7:28; 11:1; 13:53; 19:1; 26:1)**.

Why are there five collections? Because the author was seeking to show that Jesus was the new law-giver, the true successor of Moses, whose laws were contained in the first five books of the Old

Testament. It is a similar message to the one implicit in the account of Jesus' transfiguration. If you recall, Jesus was seen by the disciples talking to Moses, the great law-giver, and Elijah, the great prophet. Then a cloud passes over them and Jesus is left alone and the disciples are told:

> *'This is my Son, my Beloved . . .* ***listen to him.****'* **(Matthew 17:5 [my emphasis])**

That is the contention of Matthew's gospel—we need to listen to him. His laws are now binding on us. The future belongs to him.

Whoever the gospel writer was, he was Jewish, and he sought to show that in every jot and tittle Jesus was the Messiah to which Jewish literature had pointed. The fact that he had been rejected by his own people was the reason why the temple was now a heap of rubble! In line after seering line, the author demonstrates that Jewish leaders were responsible for murdering their own Messiah by their hypocrisy, self-indulgence and cant. For generations they had been straining away at insignificant details and had been blind to the truth that had been staring them in the face. Roman soldiers may have erected the cross, but Jews bore the guilt. It is this gospel writer who puts into Jewish mouths those dreadful words:

> *'His blood be upon us, and on our children.'* **(Matthew 27:25)**

With the dust of the fallen temple still in the air, the author of Matthew's gospel hammers out his faith before Jewish opponents, convinced that the law and the Old Testament now belong to the Christians.

77 Luke

Luke 1–24; 'We' passages: Acts 16:6-40; 20:6–28

DOCTOR Luke's contribution to the life of the early Church was considerable. He was a friend of Paul, and played an important part in the apostle's decision to take the gospel from Troas to Philippi, thus bringing Christianity to Europe. He was not Paul's constant companion, but as the 'we' passages of Acts show, he did join him from time to time, keeping a diary of the experiences they shared. He was a very gifted writer whose graphic description of Paul's journey to Rome and the subsequent shipwreck off the coast of Malta is better than anything in Robinson Crusoe.

It was Luke who had the idea to write an account of the way Christianity had spread from humble beginnings in Bethlehem to the provincial capital Jerusalem, and from there to the centre of the world—Rome itself. His gospel and Acts of Apostles, both dedicated to Theophilus, are the only comprehensive pictures we have of the early development of Christianity. Because of the sweep of his work and his accurate references to officials in Roman administrations, Luke has long been regarded as the 'historian' of the early Church. Only more recently has he been seen as a self-conscious theologian who was interested in history only insofar as it involved the salvation of mankind. This history is in three stages:

1. The period of Israel from Adam to John the Baptist
2. The ministry of Jesus, which is the centre of all history
3. The period of the Church that looks backwards to the time of salvation and forward to the second coming of Jesus and the climax of all things

Unlike Matthew, who confines himself to Israel's response to Jesus, Luke is at pains to show the universal nature of Christianity. A characteristic of his work is to indicate how the 'man from Nazareth' appealed to Gentiles as well as Jews. Luke tells us that Jesus healed a Samaritan of leprosy, visited Samaritan villages and made one of their number the hero of a parable. We are told that a Roman centurion was commended for his faith which was greater than anything Jesus had found in Israel. Another feature of Luke's writing is the way he points out the special concern Jesus had for the underprivileged, the oppressed and the ostracised. Having been born in squalor and welcomed into the world by shepherds on the night shift, Jesus, for the rest of his life, forms a kinship with publicans and sinners. The chosen may not respond to his invitation, but the poor, the maimed, the blind, the lame, do respond to him gladly. For down-and-outs, like Lazarus, who are at the bottom of the social heap, the future is alive with hope but it is laden with doom for the rich who despise the poor. Jesus' tenderest words are reserved for those who have lost their way, like the prostitute who washes his feet, the prodigal son who squanders his father's wealth and the repentant tax collector who was so ashamed of his life that he could not lift his head in the temple. All shunned Zacchaeus the quisling, but Jesus accepted his hospitality; women were second-class citizens but Jesus elevated them to important positions in his mission; at his own death Jesus has a word of encouragement for a fellow-sufferer on the cross.

Luke also portrays Jesus as a man of prayer. He prays often, usually alone and sometimes throughout the night. At the extremities of experience, such as his baptism and arrest, he prays. He tells parables about prayer and spends time teaching his followers how to pray. In no other gospel is the note of praise and thanksgiving so frequently struck, and it is Luke who incorporates into his work the great songs from the liturgy of primitive Christian worship.

Luke's achievement was truly remarkable. Fusing Mark's gospel with collected saying of Jesus and his own unique source, he presented Jesus as the Jewish Messiah *and* the hope of the *world*. Nobody was excluded from the limits of God's love—no man or woman, no slave or freedman, no Jew or Gentile, no harlot or soldier, for His arms embraced the world. It was Luke who most beautifully depicted the life of Jesus and then went on to describe how that life ultimately soaked into the heart of the Roman Empire.

78 John

John 1–21; the three letters of John

THE work of evangelists such as Paul, Peter, Barnabas, Philip and Silas had vigorously taken Christianity beyond Palestine. Like new wine bursting out of old wineskins, it shook off the restraints of Judaism and challenged the beliefs of the Graeco-Roman world. When Jerusalem was destroyed in 70 AD, Christianity already had a strong foothold in Rome and was being whispered in the sculleries and stables of the Emperor's household.

The faith was still expressed in Jewish terms and it became imperative that it should be re-interpreted for more sophisticated Gentiles who could not accept Jewish ideas of Messiahship. Paul had already preached Christianity in European cities such as Athens and Rome with some success, but the need was for a truly Gentile gospel. Then, towards the end of the first century, a man called John, who lived in the major Christian centre of Ephesus in Asia Minor, and who had known the apostle John, wrote another Gospel. He did not repeat the story of Jesus as found in Mark, Matthew and Luke, but gave a theological interpretation of that life. He was familiar with the traditions about Jesus, but sought to give them a deeper meaning as seen through the eyes of faith. At the same time he tried to make Jesus understandable and relevant to a brave new world by making his gospel a bridge between Jewish Christianity and the Gentiles.

It was not a completely new idea, and Philo, a Jewish philosopher from Alexandria, had already tried to popularise Judaism by retelling Old Testament stories and interpreting them in symbolic and allegorical fashion. On the other hand, Greek ideas had crossed the bridge in the opposite direction, making some Jews familiar with Greek philosophy. These included Gnosticism, a belief that the world we live in with its mixture of light and darkness, good and evil, spirit and matter, was inferior to a higher world, where light and goodness and spirit prevailed. These Gnostics claimed that some 'spiritual beings' could escape the prison of this world through knowledge and through a redeemer who would come from the higher world.

In John's gospel, Jesus is the one who comes from this higher world and becomes 'the Word' or 'the Logos', a term known to Greeks who regarded the Logos as the creative force of God. John's claim, therefore, was that this creative force of God had become a man and lived among us. The simple teaching of the first three gospels is transformed into philosophy, and Jesus the teller of parables becomes a more abstract philosopher. Thus he is depicted as bread that will nourish the hungry world forever; he is light for a world badly in need of someone to illuminate those born blind; he is both shepherd and sacrificial lamb who takes away the sin of the world; he is the true suffering servant who washes his disciples' feet. Jesus' ministry becomes a series of 'signs' for those with eyes to see water changed into wine, and thousands nourished by the simple sharing of a few loaves and fish. The 'signs' reach a climax when the story of Lazarus reveals Jesus to be lord of the living and the dead.

John's work reads like a first-century 'passion play', for he uses characters only insofar as they illustrate his message. When Judas, the betrayer, had received the bread at the last supper he went out. *It was night!* When Roman soldiers clothe Jesus with a crown of thorns and purple robe, Pilate, the procurator cried, *Behold the man!* When a forlorn Peter is confirmed as the first leader of the believers, his commission was, *Feed my sheep!*

At Antioch in Syria the popularity of Matthew's gospel persisted, but in Asia Minor the dramatic style of John made his gospel the firm favourite. In other areas, a blended version of the four gospels had some attraction until eventually the collection of all four became universal practice.

No doubt there were many other 'lives of Jesus' written in the first century and hundreds of letter and documents, but years later after much disagreement, the believers agreed on a selection of written material that was capable of pointing people to Jesus, who, they were convinced, was not just the Jewish Messiah, but

The image of the invisible God.

79 *John's Revelation*

Revelation 1–22

IN the first years of Christianity, strongest opposition came from Jews who did not accept that Jesus was their Messiah. Paul and other evangelists found themselves in constant conflict with Jewish leaders who opposed them at every turn. Such was their determination to silence Paul that he had to fall back on his rights as a Roman citizen to get a fair trial. This situation changed dramatically, however, when Emperor Nero came to the purple. Claudius had expelled some Christians from Rome, but it was Nero who, after a disastrous fire in the city, tried to remove suspicion from himself by blaming the Christians. The Roman historian Tacitus said:

> *Nero fastened the guilt and inflicted the most exquisite tortures on a class hated for their abominations called Christians by the populus* (***Annals*** **XV.44**).

Nero's conduct raised some feelings of pity for the Christians who, according to Tacitus, were seen to be suffering not so much for the public good as to gratify the cruelty of an individual.

The persecution of Nero, which probably brought to an end the lives of Peter and Paul, was a precedent that was to be followed intermittently for the next 250 years. It was not constant persecution, but the threat was always there, leading a second-century Christian called Tertullian to remark:

> *If the Tiber rises too high or the Nile too low, the cry is: 'The Christians to the lions'* (***Apologeticum I,*** **CXXXVII**).

The deep-seated enmity that developed between Empire and Church was not typical of Roman justice, which was usually very tolerant of foreign worship. The great difference was that the Christians could not, and would not, stomach the concept that a Roman Caesar could somehow be a god. From the days of Octavius Augustus, sacrifices had been offered to the emperors who became the embodiment of the genius of Rome, and citizens usually acquiesced in the practice. Christians did not. Furthermore, Roman government became paranoid about private organisations which, they thought, might contain within them the seeds of rebellion. One emperor even banned the meeting of his fire brigade! Because Christians met secretly, refused to sacrifice to the emperor and sometimes declined to serve in the army, they were particularly suspect.

About 95 AD, the Emperor Domitian began a persecution of Christians that led to the death of his own cousin Flavius Clemens and the banishment of Clemens' wife, Domitilla. It also led to the exile of a man called John who was left on the small barren island of Patmos, in the Aegean Sea. While on this island, he reflected strongly on the dangers facing the vulnerable Churches of Asia where emperor worship was vigorously applied. He decided to write a letter of encouragement to them using a similar style to that used in the Old Testament book of Daniel, which had so strengthened Jewish resistance to Antiochus Ephiphanes. That letter, now called the book of Revelation, is the last book of the New Testament and is probably the most abused book in the Bible.

In vivid and dramatic visions John describes the hostile forces marshalled against Christ and his Church. Pages are filled with cryptic symbols of dragons and beasts thirsting for the blood of the saints. One beast blasphemes against God and wages war upon God's people to such an extent that the whole world seems to follow after him. Another beast (probably Nero), long thought dead, returns to life and images are built to honour him, and all those who refuse are killed. It is a time of dreadful hardship and woe recounted in symbols of swords, eyes, trumpets, horns, seals and numbers, but throughout there is a recurring theme of hope. Tyranny may reign,

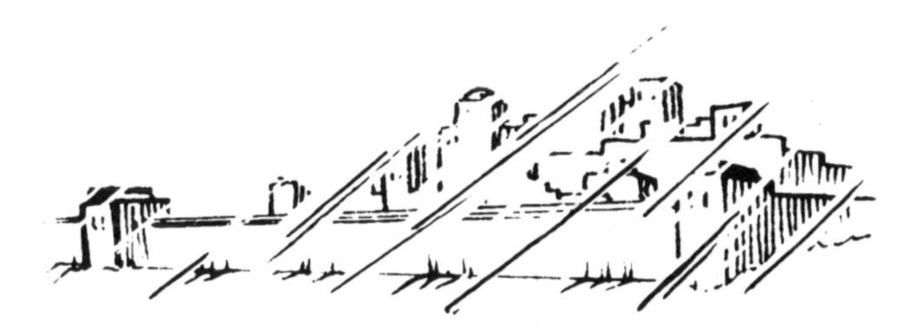

A new Jerusalem will be established.

but not forever. Soon the eternal sovereignty of Christ will be established, tribulation will be turned to glory and soon a new Jerusalem will be established, inhabited by ransomed and faultless people. At last God will have his dwelling with men.

> *He will dwell among them and they shall be his people, and God himself will be with them. He will wipe every tear from their eyes; there shall be an end to death, and to mourning and crying and pain; for the old order has passed away!* **(Revelation 21:3-4)**

John's letter, weird though it might seem to us, is a message of hope to people weary of the struggle against oppression and saddened by the deaths of their leaders. When it seemed that lamps were going out all over the world, John's letter from Patmos brought consolation and hope to the beleaguered, as it has done to countless generations since.

80 Postscript

SO this catalogue of biblical characters comes to a close. However, it does not end here, for the saga to which they made their unique contribution goes on, and the faith to which most of them testified has been taken up by others. To paraphrase the writer of Hebrews:

> *Time is too short for me to tell the stories of Polycarp, Augustine, Francis of Assisi, John Wycliffe, Martin Luther, Ignatius Loyola, John Wesley, William Carey and David Ben-Gurion. Through faith they overthrew kingdoms, established justice, saw God's promises fulfilled* **(adapted from Hebrews 11:32-33).**

In other words, the inspiration of Abraham and Moses, rekindled by the prophets and renewed by Jesus, continues to the present time. Were it possible to continue Acts of the Apostles or the Testaments of the Patriarchs, '. . . I suppose the whole world could not hold the books that would be written' (John 21:25).

There are bleak periods of history when the flame of inspiration flickers so weakly it seems certain to be extinguished, as in the days of Emperor Nero or, more recently, Emperor Stalin, but then it flares up again with new vigour and hope. There are also times when we seem capable of convincing ourselves that mankind is moving along in some inexorable march towards progress, from barbarism to Utopia, until a Nazi era or the pogroms of modern warfare remind us of the fundamental flaw in human nature that keeps 'the wheel of our existence red-hot' (James 3:6).

For long enough, people living under democratic rule have looked to governments to bring prosperity and happiness to our lives. Through education and social reforms we hope for the dawning of an age of peace and tranquillity. Such an age there has never been, and all the evidence suggests that such hopes are a pipe dream.

It is time we looked again at the lives of people who made a contribution to the book we call the Bible. Here we see motives uncovered, causes followed by effects. We see Amos writing the scripts of Martin Luther King, Jeremiah, the Jewish patriot, confronting the same dilemma as the German Dietrich Bonhoeffer during the Second World War, and an exiled Ezekiel with the same aspirations as the Russian exile Alexander Solzhenitsyn. In the plan of God and in the nature of human beings, there is nothing new under the sun. Dr Alexis Carrel of the Rockefeller Institute for Medical Research wrote in *Man the Unknown**:

> *Without the Bible, history would be the spectacle of unknown rivers flowing from unknown sources to unknown seas; but under its guidance we can trace the complex currents to their springs, and see the end from the beginning.*

Not only do our faith and our ideas of right and wrong depend upon the Bible, so does our whole civilisation.

* USA: Harper Brothers, 1939.

Index of Biblical References

Old Testament

New Testament

APOCRYPHA

Index of Subjects